First published in the UK 2019 by Sona Books
an imprint of Danann Publishing Ltd.

CAT NO: SON0583
ISBN: 978-1-915343-38-3

Made in the UAE.

Welcome to
The Compact Beginner's Guide to
Knitting

In recent years we have seen a popularity boom surrounding all kinds of crafts. Once the reserve of older generations, hand-knitting skills have taken on a new life as a modern art form and relaxing pastime. So, from lavish fashion trends to homemade gifts, add a hand-crafted touch to your garments, gifts and decorations with the help of *The Compact Beginner's Guide to Knitting*. Start by choosing your yarn and needles before getting to grips with casting on, knitting, purling, ribbing and casting off again. Once you've mastered the essentials, find out how to finish projects with finesse. Next you'll put your newfound skills into practice with a range of creative project patterns that are perfect for newbie knitters. So pick up your needles today, and you'll be an expert in no time at all!

Contents

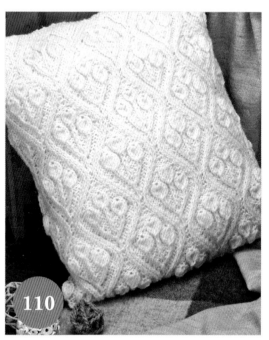

62

110

118

Getting started

80

124

Getting Started

Get to grips with the basics of knitting

"There are two things you need to get started with knitting: yarn and knitting needles"

Yarns

From chunky wool to 4-ply acrylic, there is a wide variety of yarns with which you can knit

To begin knitting, it's pretty straightforward, as all you need are two things: a pair of knitting needles and a ball of yarn. The yarn that you decide to use will play a part in determining which needles you work with, so let's start by looking at the many types of yarn available to you.

Yarns are made with a wide variety of fibres; most are natural, some are synthetic, and others blend different fibres together. All yarns have different textures and properties, and will affect the look and feel of your finished project. For example, wool is stretchy and

tough, alpaca is soft and luxurious, and natural and synthetic blends are durable with other enhanced properties.

When choosing a yarn you also need to consider its thickness, usually called its weight. Different weights affect the appearance of your project and the number of stitches needed.

When learning to knit, it's a good idea to start with a medium-weight yarn that feels comfortable in your hand and is smooth but not too slippery. A yarn described as worsted, Aran or 10-ply in wool or a wool blend is ideal.

Wool
Wool is very warm and tough, which makes it great for winter wear. It can be fine and soft or rough and scratchy, but will soften with washing. It's mostly affordable, durable and a good choice for the new knitter.

Cotton
This natural vegetable fibre is typically less elastic than wool, and is known for its robustness and washability. Cotton has a lovely stitch definition when knitted, and is good for homewares and bags. However, it can be a bit hard on the hands.

Mohair
Mohair is a silk-like fibre that comes from the Angora goat. It's a yarn that dyes particularly well and is commonly blended with other fibres. It makes for fantastic winter garments as it is warm and durable.

Acrylic
Made from polyacrylonitrile, acrylic yarn is both affordable and also washable. This synthetic yarn is very soft to the touch and comes in a wide variety of colours and textures. Acrylic is commonly blended with other yarns in order to add durability.

Alpaca
With long and fine fibres, alpaca yarn can sometimes be hairy looking, but it is one of the warmest and most luxurious wools out there. It is also incredibly soft, and comes in varieties such as baby and royal, which are even softer.

Natural and synthetic blends
Blending natural and man-made fibres often creates yarns that are stronger and more versatile. It can also enhance their appearance, making them shinier or more vibrant. Blended yarns are often washable, making them great for garments for children.

Did you know?

Every ball of yarn comes with a recommended needle size, which is printed on the label. Use bigger needles than this to make a more open stitch, and smaller ones to make a tighter, more compact fabric.

Yarn Weights

Yarn weight	Properties	Ideal for	Recommended needle sizes		
			Metric	US	Old UK
Lace, 2-ply, fingering	Extremely light, Lace yarn produces a very delicate knit on 2mm (US 0) needles. Bigger needles will produce a more open fabric.	Lace	2mm 2.25mm 2.5mm	0 1	14 13
Superfine, 3-ply, fingering, baby	Using very slim needles, Superfine yarn is perfect for lightweight, intricate lace work.	Fine-knit socks, shawls, babywear	2.75mm 3mm 3.25mm	2 3	12 11 10
Fine, 4-ply, sport, baby	Fine yarn is great for socks, and can also be used in items that feature slightly more delicate textures.	Light jumpers, babywear, socks, accessories	3.5mm 3.75mm 4mm	4 5 6	 9 8
Double knit (DK), light worsted, 5/6-ply	An extremely versatile weight yarn, DK can be used to create a wide variety of things and knits up relatively quickly.	Jumpers, light-weight scarves, blankets, toys	4mm 4.5mm	7	7
Aran, medium worsted, Afghan, 12-ply	With many yarns in this thickness using a variety of fibres to make them machine washable, Aran yarn is good for garments with thick cabled detail and functional items.	Jumpers, cabled garments, blankets, hats, scarves, mittens	5mm 5.5mm	8 9	6 5
Chunky, bulky, craft, rug, 14-ply	Quick to knit, chunky yarn is perfect for warm outerwear. Often made from lightweight fibres to prevent drooping.	Rugs, jackets, blankets, hats, legwarmers, winter accessories	6mm 6.5mm 7mm 8mm	10 10.5 11	4 3 2 0
Super chunky, super bulky, bulky, roving, 16-ply and upwards	Commonly used with very large needles, Super chunky yarn knits up very quickly. Good for beginners as large stitches make mistakes easy to spot.	Heavy blankets, rugs, thick scarves	9mm 10mm	13 15	00 000

Knitting needles

The tools of the trade, choosing your needles will ultimately depend on your project, yarn and, of course, personal preference

Knitting needles come in many types, sizes and materials. Once you become more familiar with knitting, you may find that you prefer one type over another, but the variations are designed with different patterns and yarns in mind. This guide will explain the features of each, but the best way to decide which needles suit you is to practise and find the ones that feel most comfortable.

Learning to knit on bent, dull or rough needles will be a frustrating process, so it's worth investing in a good pair that feel nice in your hands to get started. To practise knitting, it's better to work with thick yarn as this will make it easier to spot mistakes. If you're getting started with yarn that is Aran weight or thicker, your first pair of needles should be at least 5mm (US 8) in diameter.

Straight needles

Pointed at one end with a stopper at the other, straight knitting needles come in pairs and a variety of lengths. Short needles are best for small projects and long needles are recommended for wider projects, such as blankets. When you're new to knitting, it's best to start with long, straight needles, as they have more length to hold on to and give the most support to the hand.

Metal needles

Strong and not prone to bending, metal needles are good for all types of yarns, especially wool, wool blends and acrylic. Stitches move quickly on the polished surface of metal needles, which makes them quick to knit with but also unsuitable for beginners, as stitches can easily slip off the needle's tip. Metal needles of more than 8mm (US 11) in diameter can be heavy and difficult to work with.

Plastic needles

Lightweight and flexible, plastic needles can be used with all types of yarns. The smooth surface of plastic needles allows stitches to move quickly, but not as quickly as on metal needles, so the risk of stitches slipping off the needle is reduced. Larger needles are commonly made of plastic in order to reduce their weight.

Bamboo needles

Bamboo needles are strong and tend to be lighter than metal needles. The bamboo has a slight grip, which helps to keep stitches regularly spaced, creating an even knit. This also minimises the risk of stitches slipping off the needle's tip, making them an excellent choice for beginners. Bamboo needles are also recommended for arthritis sufferers, as they are warm to the touch and can warp slightly to fit the curvature of the hand.

Square needles

Although most needles are cylindrical, square needles with four flat sides make a more consistent stitch and require less hand tension to maintain in position. This makes them good for beginners and arthritis sufferers.

Image credit: KnitPro

Double-pointed and circular needles

In order to produce a tube of knitting without a seam, such as a sock or cowl, you will need to knit in the round using double-pointed or circular needles. Choosing which to use will often depend on the length of your project. Double-pointed needles (DPNs) can knit a very narrow tube, whereas circular needles are better for larger projects.

Double-pointed needles

Usually sold in sets of four or five, double-pointed needles (DPNs) have points at both ends. They are typically quite short and do not hold a lot of stitches, so are best for smaller projects, such as socks.

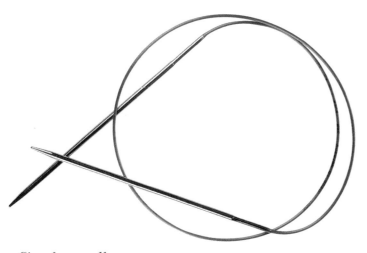

Circular needles

These are two straight needles connected with a flexible plastic cord. The cord can come in many different lengths, from 30-152cm (12-60in), and it is important to choose a length that is appropriate for your project. A good rule of thumb is to use a cord that will match or be slightly smaller than the circumference of the piece you are knitting.

Size

Knitting needles come in a variety of diameters, from as small as 1.5mm (US 000 / 00) up to 25mm (US 50). The size of the needle that you use will determine the size of the stitch you create, and most yarns will come with a recommended needle size.

There are three common needle-sizing systems: European metric, old British and American. Use this chart to convert between sizes. If your needles are not labelled by diameter, you may need to buy a needle size gauge to establish their size.

Metric (mm)	US	Old UK
1.5	000 / 00	N/A
2	0	14
2.25 / 2.5	1	13
2.75	2	12
3	N/A	11
3.25	3	10
3.5	4	N/A
3.75	5	9
4	6	8
4.5	7	7
5	8	6
5.5	9	5
6	10	4
6.5	10.5	3
7	N/A	2
7.5	N/A	1
8	11	0
9	13	00
10	15	000
12	17	N/A
15	19	N/A
20	35	N/A
25	50	N/A

Knitting kit bag

Although you can quite easily start knitting with just a pair of needles and a ball of yarn, there are lots of other useful tools available

Needle organiser

When you've built up a collection of needles of all different sizes and types, storing them can become tricky. A needle organiser keeps them all in one place and protected against damage. Depending on your preference, you can get either a needle roll or a bag, which is like a long pencil case.

Row counter

Used to keep track of how many rows you've knitted, this is another helpful tool that will save you from counting the stitches in your work. There are different types of counters available; some sit on the end of your needle and can be turned at the end of each row, while others are available as a clicker.

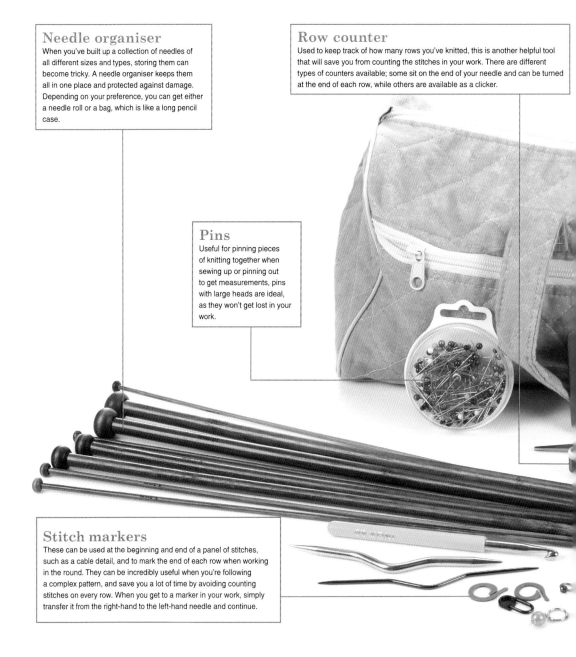

Pins

Useful for pinning pieces of knitting together when sewing up or pinning out to get measurements, pins with large heads are ideal, as they won't get lost in your work.

Stitch markers

These can be used at the beginning and end of a panel of stitches, such as a cable detail, and to mark the end of each row when working in the round. They can be incredibly useful when you're following a complex pattern, and save you a lot of time by avoiding counting stitches on every row. When you get to a marker in your work, simply transfer it from the right-hand to the left-hand needle and continue.

Knitting bag

Available at most craft stores, knitting bags come with many compartments for storing all your tools and materials. They are usually made of sturdy material that won't be damaged by the sharp points of your needles.

Did you know?

Knitting is actually good for your health. Studies have proven that knitting can help reduce blood pressure, decrease heart rate, and provide many benefits for those suffering with mental health issues.

Point protectors

These will prevent the points of your needles from being damaged, as well as other things being damaged by them. Sharp needles will easily puncture bags, and fragile tips can be rather prone to breaking while being transported. Point protectors will also prevent unfinished work from slipping off the ends of your needles while you are not working on your project.

Knitting needle gauge

It's essential to know what size of needle you're knitting with. If you're unsure, either because the needle has no marking or it has been rubbed off, a needle gauge will be able to tell you. All you need to do is poke the needle through the holes to find the best fit. Most will also feature a ruler to measure tension squares.

Scissors

You will need a pair of scissors for cutting off yarn and trimming edges. It's best to use a good-quality pair with sharp, short blades that will allow you to snip close to the work for a clean finish.

Stitch holders

Available in many different sizes, these are used to hold stitches that you will return to later. You can even make your own from a length of thin yarn or a safety pin.

Tape measure

A handy tool when you're knitting to exact measurements, you should always keep a tape measure nearby. Not only can you use it to measure the person you are knitting for, but also to check your tension and the size and progress of your piece of knitting.

Making a slip knot

Almost every piece that you knit will begin with this simple knot, which creates your first stitch

T his is an easy and quick-to-learn knot. The slip knot is, in fact, the first loop you will place on the needle when you begin a piece of knitting, and it will form the first stitch.

There are many ways to create a slip knot, and as you practise making it, you might find that you develop your own technique. Here is just one way.

01 Make a circle

Lay out a length of yarn. Pick it up close to the ball and cross it over the yarn end (called the tail) to make a circle.

02 Bring the yarn through

Insert the tip of a needle through the circle of yarn and underneath it, then over the piece of yarn coming from the ball end. Pull this bit of yarn through the circle.

03 Knot and loop

This forms a loop on the needle and a loose knot below, as shown in the image above.

04 Tighten

With the needle in one hand, pull both ends of the yarn firmly in order to tighten the knot and the loop.

05 Check tension

Ensure the slip knot is tight enough that it won't fall off the needle or fall apart but not so tight that you can't move it along the needle.

06 Assess the tail

The tail end of your yarn should be at least 10-15cm (4-6in) long so it can be woven in later. Some patterns will instruct that you leave a longer tail (called a long loose end) to use for seams or something else at a later stage.

Holding yarn & needles

Picking up your needles and yarn together for the first time might feel a bit awkward and unnatural, but it will soon become second nature

It will take practice to hold needles and yarn comfortably. You'll mostly hold the yarn and a needle in one hand at the same time, which can be complicated. For now, do what feels comfortable. As you improve, you will find a technique that works for you.

There are two styles of knitting: holding the yarn in the right hand is called English style and holding it in the left hand is called Continental style. However, knitting is ambidextrous, so whether you're right or left handed, try both to see which you prefer. technique. Here is just one way.

English style

01 Position the yarn
With your palm facing you, wrap the yarn around your little finger on your right hand. Take it across your next two fingers then under your index finger. You need to control the yarn firmly but with a relaxed hand, so that the yarn will flow through your fingers as you knit.

02 Alternative technique
If you can't get comfortable, try this technique, or any other that you prefer, instead. The main thing you need to make sure of is that the tension is enough to create even loops that are not too loose or too tight. Keep this in mind the whole time.

03 Hold the needles
Once your yarn is in position, grab your needles. The needle with the stitches about to be worked needs to be in the left hand, and the other in the right. Use the right index finger (or middle finger if you prefer) to wrap the yarn around the needle.

Continental style

01 Position the yarn
Wrap the yarn around your little finger with your palm facing you. Then take it over the next two fingers to lace it underneath your index finger. Check your tension: not too loose and not too tight.

02 Alternative technique
If that does not feel comfortable, try wrapping the yarn around a different finger. You can also try wrapping the yarn twice around the index finger, which will help you tighten the tension if you need to.

03 Hold the needles
As with English-style knitting, hold the needle with the stitches to be worked in the left hand and the other in the right. Use your left index finger to wrap the yarn around the right-hand needle when working a stitch.

Casting (binding) on

**Now you're comfortable holding your needles and yarn,
it's time to get knitting. The first step is casting on**

To get started, you must cast (bind) on. This creates a row of loops that will be the foundation for your knitting. There are many methods. Single-strand cast (bind) ons are simple and soft; they can be created using one or two needles. Two-strand cast (bind) ons mostly use one needle and are strong, elastic and versatile.

Here, we are going to showcase three of the most common cast (bind) ons, but there is an abundance of others with different properties that you can also use, and which will affect the look of your knitting. Don't forget to create your first stitch with a slip knot — turn back to page 14 if you need a reminder on how to do this.

01 Make a loop around your thumb

This is the simplest cast (bind) on, and is quick and easy to get on the needle. With the needle that has the slip knot on it in your right hand, wrap the working yarn around your left-hand thumb (and index finger if it's more comfortable). Hold the yarn in place in your palm.

02 Collect the loop

Put the needle tip near the crook of your thumb and underneath the yarn that is closest to you. Pull it up so that the yarn is on the needle.

03 Tighten the stitch

Pull the loop off your thumb (and index finger if necessary) with the needle, but keep hold of the yarn in the palm of your hand. Lift the needle or pull on the yarn to tighten the stitch.

04 Repeat the process

Wrap the yarn around your left-hand thumb again and continue making loops until you have the desired number on your needle.

Cable cast (bind) on
Master this casting (binding) on alternative

01 Begin to knit
Holding the yarn in either English or Continental style, place the needle with the slip knot in your left hand. Put the tip of the right-hand needle through the loop on the left needle.

02 Make a loop
With the yarn behind the needles, wrap it under and around the right needle. With the tip of the right needle, carefully pull the yarn through the loop on the left needle.

03 Transfer to the needle
To move the loop from the right needle to the left, insert the tip of the left needle from right to left through the front of the loop. Tighten the loop by pulling both yarn ends.

04 Insert the needle
Put the tip of the right needle between the two loops on the left needle. Then, you must wrap the yarn under and around the tip of the right needle.

05 Pull the loop through
Now you need to draw the yarn through very carefully with the tip of the right needle. You should find that you have a loop on the right-hand needle.

06 Continue
Move the loop on the right needle to the left as you did in step 3. Continue, being sure to insert the needle between the first two loops on the left needle.

Long tail cast (bind) on
Create an even, stretchy edge with this cast (bind) on

01 Leave a tail
This cast (bind) on is a bit harder, as it uses two yarn strands (the working yarn and the tail) at the same time. You will need to use a long tail, one that is approximately four times as long as the desired width of your cast (bind) on. Start by holding the needle with the slip knot in your right hand. In your left hand, hold the tail going over your thumb and the working yarn over your index finger. Hold both strands in your palm.

02 Pick up the loop
Insert the tip of the needle under the loop on your thumb, much the same as when making the single cast (bind) on.

03 Go over the back
While keeping the yarn on your thumb, wrap the tip of the needle around the loop on your index finger.

04 Form the first stitch
Pull the yarn through the space next to your thumb and then up to form a stitch.

05 Tighten the stitch
Release the yarn from your thumb and pull both ends to tighten the stitch on the needle.

06 Continue the process
Loop the strands of yarn around your thumb and index finger again, and repeat the steps until you have the desired number of stitches.

Did you know?

If you have wooden knitting needles, it's very important to clean and moisturise them once or twice a year using natural wax wood cleaners.

The knit stitch

Learn the foundation stitch of knitting with this simple tutorial and you'll be making scarves, tea cosies and more in next to no time

The knit stitch (abbreviated as K in patterns) is the very first stitch that you'll learn. It is the most important stitch and even when it's used on its own you can still create great pieces from scarves to tea cosies. Now that you've learnt how to cast (bind) on — we recommend that you start off with cable cast (bind) on (page 17) — you're more than 80 per cent of the way there with knit stitch.

Working the knit stitch (K) every row is called garter stitch (g st), the result is a flat fabric with horizontal ridges of V stitches and bumps, this somewhat corrugated finish is great for making warm garments as the rows of bumps hold in warm air. Garter stitch is also often worked on the edges of flat pieces of stocking (stockinette) stitch (st st) knitting to prevent it from curling. Once you've followed the steps and mastered the stitch, have a go at the garter stitch scarf.

"It's the most important stitch — even when it's used on its own you can still create great pieces"

Knit stitch
Discover how to master the knit stitch

01 Use the cable cast (bind) on method
Following the cable cast (bind) on method on page 17, cast (bind) on a manageable 20 stitches. Hold the needle with your stitches in your left hand and with your right hand hold the yarn at the back of your needles, insert the point of right-hand needle into the left side of first stitch (loop) on the left-hand needle.

02 Maintain an even tension (gauge)
With the yarn guided by your index finger, wind it under and around the point of the right-hand needle, in an anti-clockwise direction. Keep the yarn in your right hand relatively taut, this will help to keep your work stable and maintain an even tension (gauge).

03 Thread the needle through the loop
With a firm hold of the left-hand needle, carefully move the right-hand needle so that you bring the tip through the loop on the left-hand needle, catching the yarn that you wound round the needle in step 1.

04 Finish the stitch
Move the right-hand needle little further through the stitch that you have just created, then gently pulling the right needle to your right, you can let the stitch from the left needle drop off. You have now worked one knit (K) stitch. Continue for the rest of the row. When you've worked all the stitches, swap the needles into the other hands and start again.

Cast (bind) off knitwise
Learn how to cast off kwise

01 Begin to cast (bind) off
With the yarn at the back of the work knit the first two stitches as you
would normally do. Then insert the tip of the left-hand needle into the
right side of the first stitch on the right-hand needle.

02 One stitch at a time
Lift the stitch over the second stitch and the tip of the right-hand needle
then drop from the left needle. You have cast (bind) off one stitch. Knit
the next stitch and repeat to the end of the row.

03 Loop and pull
At the end of the row you will be left with one stitch on the right needle.
Cut your yarn to leave a tail of approximately 15cm (8in) and enlarge the
last stitch and feed the end of the yarn through the loop and pull tightly.

Garter stitch scarf

Pick an interesting yarn with texture and colour variations in order to make a creative garter stitch scarf

While garter stitch is a simple stitch, it looks most effective when worked in an interesting yarn. Here we've chosen a super snuggly, super chunky weight yarn that has texture and subtle colour differences.

Difficulty ★☆☆☆☆

Skills needed
Knitting in rows

Finished measurements
152cm (60in)

Yarn
For this pattern you will need a super chunky yarn. In the example Sirdar Bohemia was used in Ombre. You will need approximately 135m (147yd) for the main body of the scarf, plus more for tassels.

Tension (Gauge)
7 stitches and 10 rows = 10x10cm (4x4in) in garter stitch using 15mm (US 19) needles, or size required to obtain correct tension (gauge).

Needles
15mm (US 19) needles

Other supplies
Crochet hook for tassels

Construction notes
You'll need to add in new balls of yarn for this project. Turn to page 32 to see how to do this, then turn to page 81 to find out how to darn in the ends.

Garter stitch scarf
Using 15mm needles, cast (bind) on 14 sts leaving a long tail.

Row 1: Knit.

Continue to knit every row until you have worked all three balls of yarn leaving enough to cast (bind) off or have a scarf the length that you require.

Add your new balls at the start of the row.

Cast (bind) off knitwise and cut the yarn leaving a long tail.

Note: If you prefer a narrower scarf, cast (bind) on fewer stitches. Similarly, to make a wider scarf, cast (bind) on more stitches.

Making up
Darn in yarn tails, however if you are adding tassels to your scarf, there is no need to darn in the cast (bind) on and cast (bind) off tails of yarn.

Making tassels

01 Wind your yarn loosely around an object to obtain the length you require.

02 Cut the yarn along the bottom edge. You will now have lengths of yarn. Be careful to keep them all the same length.

03 Taking two strands of yarn, insert your crochet hook into the end of the scarf, catch the middle of the yarn on the hook and pull through the knitting to make a loop.

04 Feed the four yarn ends through the loop and pull tight. Repeat this to add more tassels at equal intervals along both ends of the scarf. Once you have added all the tassels, cut all to the same length.

The purl stitch

Now that you have mastered the knit stitch, it's time to learn how to work its partner the purl stitch — you'll find it's not all that different

There are only two main stitches to the art of knitting. The first is knit (K), which you will have now mastered; the second is purl (P), which we will show you how to work here. When worked together with subtle variations, you will be able to make anything!

Purl stitch is effectively the reverse way to work a knit stitch. If you were to purl every row, you would end up with a piece of fabric identical to a garter stitch (g st) (knit stitch every row). However, when you work a row of knit stitches followed by a row of purl stitches and repeat these two rows, you will have a piece of fabric that has smooth 'Vs' on one side and rugged 'bumps' on the other. This is called a stocking (stockinette) stitch (st st), and you will recognise this as the standard knit fabric. Usually the 'V' side is called the right side (RS), and when this faces you on the left needle, it indicates that you knit the next row. The wrong side (WS) has bumps and indicates that you purl the next row.

When you knit a sample of stocking (stockinette) stitch, it has a tendency to curl on itself, so it is often worked alongside garter stitch (see page 20) for flat pieces and rib stitch (see page 28) for garments.

> "The WS has bumps and indicates you purl the next row"

01 Set up the needles
With the needle holding the unworked stitches in your left hand (LH) and the empty needle in your right hand (RH), hold the yarn at the front of your work. Insert the tip of the right-hand needle into the first stitch entering the loop from left to right.

02 Wind the yarn
Wind the yarn around the tip of the right needle, moving it from right to left in an anticlockwise direction, ensuring that you're keeping a tension on the yarn as it moves through your fingers.

"When worked together with subtle variations, you will be able to make anything!"

03 Work the stitches
Work the tip of the right-hand needle through the stitch on the left needle, catching the yarn as you go and drawing it through.

Reverse stocking stitch
While on the majority of patterns, a stocking stitch (st st) shows the 'V' side as the right side of your work, sometimes reverse stocking (stockinette) stitch is called for in the design. This is simply where the 'bumpy' side becomes the right side.

04 Drop off and continue
Move the right-hand needle a little further through the stitch that you have just created, then gently pulling the right needle to your right, you can let the stitch from the left needle drop off. You have now worked 1 purl (P) stitch. Continue for the rest of the row.

Cast (bind) off purlwise (p-wise)
Sometimes a pattern will ask you to cast (bind) off on a purl row

01 Purl the first 2 stitches
With the yarn at the front of the work, purl (P) the first 2 stitches as you would normally do. Then, insert the tip of the left-hand needle into the right side of the first stitch on the right-hand needle.

02 Cast and purl
Carefully lift the stitch over the second stitch and the tip of the right-hand needle, and drop from the left needle. You have cast off 1 stitch. Purl the next stitch and repeat this method to the end of the row.

03 Cut and enlarge
At the end of the row, you will be left with 1 stitch on the right needle. Cut your yarn to leave a tail of approximately 15cm (8in). Enlarge the last stitch, feed the end of the yarn through the loop and pull tightly.

Simple cushion

This stocking stitch cushion project will help you to learn the feel of the yarn and needles as well as giving you the opportunity to grasp the technique and create an even tension (gauge)

Difficulty ★☆☆☆☆

Skills needed

Knitting in rows
Stocking (stockinette) stitch
Seaming

Finished measurements

Cushion covers measures 33 x 33cm
(13 x 13 in) for a 36 x 36 cm (14 x 14 in)
cushion pad.

Yarn

For this project you will need a DK yarn. In
this example, Adriafil, Knitcol has been used
in Pascal Fancy. You will need approximately
250m (274 yd).

Tension (Gauge)

18st and 25 rows = 10cm (4in) in st st using
4.5mm (US 7) needles, or size required in
order to obtain the correct tension (gauge).

Needles

4.5mm (US 7) needles

Other supplies

Tapestry needle

Simple cushion

Cast (bind) on 60 stitches.
***Row 1 (RS)**: Knit.*
***Row 2:** Purl.*
    Repeat these 2 rows until knitting measures
66cm (26in).
    Cast (bind) off.

Making up

Darn in all ends. Fold your knitted piece in
half lengthways, with right sides facing each
other. Sew together the two side edges.
Turn the cover right side out and insert the
cushion pad and sew the opening closed using
mattress stitch.

TOP TIP

Why not add further
interest to your cushion by
making tassels and attach
them to the corners.

For more confident knitters

If you're feeling more confident, start and end with 5cm (2in) of rib stitch with 66cm (26in)
of stocking (stockinette) stitch in between. When making up, fold your knitting with the right
sides facing so that one of the rib sections overlaps the other rib section plus 5cm (2in) of
the st st to make an envelope for easy cushion pad removal.

Slipping stitches

Slipping your stitches in the correct way is a technique that is important to master, because it will ensure that your knitting looks neat and professional

To slip stitches (sl st), you must displace stitches from one needle to the other. Whether it's to decrease stitches, transfer stitches to cable needles and stitch holders, or add detail in a lace pattern, you'll use this method a lot. The result is an elongated stitch with a bar across it. Depending on whether your yarn is at the front of the work before slipping the stitch will determine whether the bar is in front or behind the slipped stitch. Unless the pattern tells you to bring the yarn to the front (yf), or take it to the back (yb), leave it where it is.

There are two ways of slipping stitches: knitwise (kwise) or purlwise (pwise). Unless the pattern instructs otherwise, slip the stitch purlwise.

Slip stitches purlwise
Master this default method

01 Prepare to purl
On both right and wrong side rows, insert the tip of the right-hand needle into the first stitch (unless otherwise stated) as if to purl the stitch.

02 Work the stitches
Drop the stitch from the left needle by sliding it onto the right. Work the next stitch as instructed, being careful not to pull the yarn too tightly.

Slip stitches knitwise
For when you are instructed

01 Prepare to knit
Slip knitwise only when instructed, as this will twist the stitch. On both right and wrong side rows, insert the tip of the right-hand needle into the first stitch (unless otherwise stated) as if to knit the stitch.

02 Work the stitches
The next part of the method is the same as if you were purling. So, drop the stitch from the left needle by sliding it onto the right. Work the next stitch as instructed, being careful not to pull the yarn too tightly.

Rib stitch

Rib is an elastic stitch that is most commonly used for welts and cuffs of garments, but used in its own right can be very useful

R ib stitch gets its name from the vertical raised and indented ridges of the worked fabric. When alternate stitches of knit (K) and purl (P) are worked along a row, you will notice that it is narrower than a piece of stocking stitch (st st) worked over the same number of stitches. This is because the fabric 'draws in', resulting in an elasticity that is perfect for cuffs and waistbands.

Most often, a garment project will ask for a section of 1x1 rib at the start of all pieces; the term 1x1 simply means that you will work a regular rib section of knit 1 (K1) stitch, then purl 1 (P1) stitch all the way across the row. In the same way a double or 2x2 rib would be worked by knitting 2 (K2) stitches, then purling 2 (P2) stitches. An irregular rib pattern will often be used for a more decorative piece of knitting (2x1 rib).

> "A garment project will ask for a section of 1x1 rib at the start"

01 Knit 1 stitch

Cast (bind) on the required number of stitches as stated in the pattern, or for practice purposes, cast (bind) on 20 stitches. With yarn at the back of the work and cast (bind) on stitches on the needle in your left hand, knit 1 (K1) stitch.

TOP TIP When working a 1x1 rib on an even number of stitches, you will always work a K st first on every row. An odd number of stitches will mean you have to alternate between K and P stitches at the start of each row.

02 Work all the stitches

Your next stitch is a purl stitch, but your yarn is at the back of your work, so bring the yarn between your needles so that it is now at the front of your work. Purl (P) the next stitch. Now take the yarn back through your needles and knit the next stitch. Continue in this way until you have worked all the stitches.

03 Look for 'Vs' and 'bumps'

Now that you have worked your first row, when you turn your knitting to work the next row, you will notice that you have alternate 'Vs' and 'bumps' below the stitches on the needle. These are handy guides to know what stitch to work next. If there is a 'V', knit (K) the stitch, and if there is a 'bump', purl (P) the stitch. After a few rows you will notice columns of alternate stitches.

Ribbed gadget cosies

Keep your technology safe in these simple-to-knit cosies. Due to its stretchy nature, rib stitch is perfect for these holders, and the raised texture will help to protect screens

TOP TIP These make quick and easy gifts for loved ones. You could use several colours and even work in stripes. See how to do this on page 32.

Difficulty ★☆☆☆☆

Skills needed
Knitting in rows
Rib stitch
Cast (bind) off in rib

Finished measurements
Smart phone cosy:
To fit phone width 6-8cm (2.5-3in) snuggly
Tablet cosy:
To fit tablet width 13-18cm (5-7in) snuggly

Yarn
For this pattern you will need a DK yarn. In the example, Woolyknit.com Countryside Tweed has been used in Cheviot. One ball is enough to make both cosies.

Tension (Gauge)
29 sts and 28 rows = 10x10cm (4x4in) in rib stitch using 4mm (US 6) needles.

Needles
4mm (US 6) needles

Other supplies
Tapestry needle

Ribbed smartphone and tablet cosies
Cast (bind) on 32 sts for the smartphone cosy, or 64 sts for the tablet cosy.
Row 1: *Knit 1, purl 1, rep from * to end of row.
Repeat row 1 until knitting measures for your desired length to fit your device.
Cast (bind) off stitches in the K1, P1 rib pattern.

Making up
Darn in ends. Fold knitting in half width-wise and join seams along the cast (bind) on edge, and then down the long side of the cosy. Turn right side out and your cosy is ready to use.

Cast off in single rib
If you've been working a pattern in rib, you'll want to cast off in rib too. This is as simple as keeping to the pattern you've been working while you cast (bind) off. To do so in single ribbing, K1, P1, then remove the first stitch from the needle as you would for a standard cast off. Always move the working yarn to the back of the work before removing a stitch.

Moss (seed) stitch

Combining knit and purl stitches can create a pretty moss (seed) stitch which, when worked in conjunction with stocking stitch, looks great

Moss (seed) stitch, which is also known as seed stitch in the US, uses alternate knit (K) and purl (P) stitches to create a textured fabric. While it looks rather complicated, this is a very easy stitch to work and looks effective when worked in between sections of stocking stitch.

If you have mastered rib stitch, then the mechanics of working moss (seed) stitch is not too dissimilar. You simply alternate between knit and purl stitches along the row, then on the next row you knit above a 'bump' and purl above a 'v'. While it is worked in a similar way to rib stitch, moss (seed) stitch actually produces a flat fabric, which does not have an elastic quality, so it would not be good to use for welts or cuffs, unless a loose finish is required.

Garments worked in moss (seed) stitch tend to be a little bulkier due to the raised 'purl' bumps, making them the perfect cover-up for a cool day. Why not work up squares of the same stitch and row count in moss (seed) stitch in different colours, and join them together to make a cot blanket, or something larger if you're feeling ambitious?

> *"Garments worked in moss (seed) stitch are a little bulkier due to the raised 'purl' bumps"*

01 Mimic the rib stitch

Cast (bind) on 20 stitches. Start your first row as you would with rib stitch: K1 stitch, P1 stitch, remembering to bring your yarn back and forth through the needles between stitches, all the way to the end of the row. (Do not take yarn over the needles, otherwise you will create extra stitches and holes in your work.)

02 Knit and purl stitches

When you swap needles so that the stitches to be worked are in your left hand, you will notice alternate 'v' and 'bump' stitches. You have an even number of stitches to work so row 2 and all even numbered rows of moss (seed) stitch you will start with a purl stitch, then alternate between knit and purl stitches to the end of the row. So effectively you purl when there is a 'v' and knit when there is a 'bump'. When you have finished, cast (bind) off your work using the rib cast (bind) off (see page 28) following the pattern set.

Variations

A 2x2 moss (seed) stitch is where you K2 sts, then P2 sts along the row. The next row K the K (v) stitches, and P the P (bump) stitches. On the third row alternate the stitches, so K the P sts and P the K stitches. On the fourth row you K the K (v) stitches, and P the P 'bump' stitches again. Repeat these 4 rows for chequerboard-effect fabric.

Textured draught excluder

**Keep your rooms nice and cozy with this textured
Moss (seed) stitch draught excluder**

Difficulty ★★☆☆☆

Skills needed

Rib stitch
Stocking (stockinette) stitch
Moss (seed) stitch
Knitting in rows
Seaming
Cast (bind) off in rib

Finished measurements

66.5cm (26in). This will fit a standard door
width, but if you wish to make a longer draught
excluder, work the pattern shown between **
and ** again to add a further 17cm (18in).

Yarn

For this pattern you will need an Aran weight
yarn. In this example we have used Sirdar,
Hayfield Bonus Aran in Petrol. You will need
approximately 210m (230yd) or more if you
want to make a longer draught excluder.

Tension (Gauge)

Work 18 sts and 22 rows in st st stitch to
measure 10x10cm (4x4in) using 5mm (US
8) needles, or the size required to obtain the
correct tension.

Needles

5mm (US 8)

Other supplies

Tapestry needle
Toy stuffing (old tights or old, cut-up t-shirts
work equally well)

Textured draught excluder

Cast (bind) on 50 sts.
Row 1: *K1, P1, rep from *.
Rep row 1 a further 9 times.
**Next row (RS): Knit.
Next row (WS): Purl.
Rep last 2 rows 12 more times ending with RS
facing for next row.

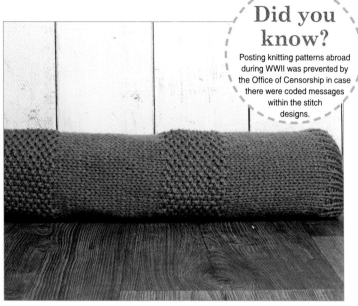

Next row: *K1, P1, rep from * to end.
Next row: *P1, K1, rep from * to end.
These 2 rows form the moss (seed) stitch.
Cont in moss (seed) stitch as set for a further
14 rows ending with RS facing for next row **.
Rep between ** and ** twice more.
Next row: Knit.
Next row: Purl.
Rep last 2 rows 12 more times.
Row 1: (K1, P1) to end of row.
Rep row 1 a further 9 times.
Cast (bind) off in rib pattern.

Making up

Darn in ends. With right sides facing, fold
the knitting in half lengthways. Join the side
edges to create a tube using a mattress stitch
(see page 98). With side edges joined and the
draught excluder inside out, flatten the tube,
so that the join is in the middle. Now join one
of the ribbed openings. Turn out the right way,
stuff with preferred material, and close final
end by oversewing the seams.

Joining a new yarn

**If your project is going to use up more than one ball of yarn,
then you will need to join the next as seamlessly as possible**

There are many things that you may like to knit in one colour that, because of their size, will need more than one ball of yarn. Joining a new ball of yarn to your existing work is very simple to do and if done well can make a seamless transition — even you won't be able to tell where you made the change.

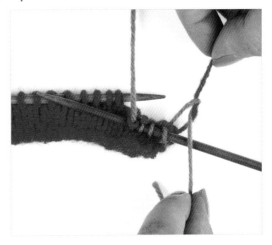

At the beginning of a row
Add a new ball of yarn to your knitting

01 Knit with the new yarn

The simplest way to join a new ball of yarn is at the beginning of a row. All you need to do is drop the old yarn and start knitting with the new. After a few stitches, tie the ends together. When you've finished the piece, darn the ends in.

In the middle of a row
Seamlessly change yarn

01 Drop the old

Sometimes it won't be possible to join the new yarn at the end of the row. If you need to join your new yarn in the middle of a row, drop the old yarn so that it rests down the back of the piece.

02 Pick up the new

In the same way as you would at the end of a row, simply start knitting with the new yarn, and after a few stitches, tie the ends together to secure them. Weave the ends in using duplicate stitch weaving when you're finished.

Felted join
Join the same colour together first

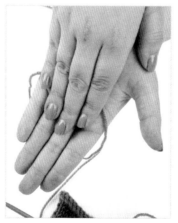

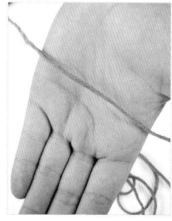

01 Pick up the ends

Although this method only works with feltable animal fibres, it will produce an almost seamless join that can be used anywhere in the row. Start by picking up the two ends of the old and new yarn and placing them in your palm, parallel to each other and heading in opposite directions. Moisten the ends with water, or simply licking your palms will do.

02 Rub them together

Between your palms, rub the two ends together firmly, but gently. The idea is to felt the fibres together using pressure, moisture and heat.

03 Knit away

The two ends will be joined. There will be a light bulge where the two have become one, but this should be barely recognisable once it is knitted into the fabric.

"This method (at the beginning of the row) can also be used to simply join a different coloured yarn, for example to incorporate a stripe along the rows."

Graduating stripes table mat

Joining a new yarn is handy in all projects, but doing so neatly when incorporating stripes into your project is paramount!

Difficulty ★☆☆☆☆

Skills needed
Moss (seed) stitch
Knitting in rows
Buttonhole

Finished measurements
Approximately 23.5cm (9.25in) long and
31.5cm (12.5in) wide.

Yarn
For this project you will need a Aran
weight yarn in various colours. In this
example the colours Teal, Light Grey and
White have been used. To make two mats,
you will need one ball of each colour.

Tension (Gauge)
18 sts and 32 rows = 10cm (4in) in moss
(seed) stitch on 4mm (US 6) needles.

Needles
4mm (US 6) needles

Other supplies
2 x 1.4mm buttons
Sewing needle and thread

Moss (seed) stitch pattern
Row 1: *K1, P1; rep from * to the last st, K1
Rep Row 1 as many times as stated.

Place Mat 1: Colour Variation 1 (Worked from the bottom up)

Using col 1, cast (bind) on 57 sts.

Rows 1-12: Work 12 rows in moss (seed) stitch. Change to col 2.

Row 13: Knit.

Rows 14-24: Work 11 rows in moss (seed) stitch. Change to col 3.

Row 25: Knit.

Rows 26-36: Work 11 rows in moss (seed) stitch. Change to col 1.

Row 37: Knit

Rows 38-46: Work 9 rows in moss (seed) stitch. Change to col 2.

Row 47: Knit.

Rows 48-56: Work 9 rows in moss (seed) stitch. Change to col 3.

Row 57: Knit.

Rows 58-66: Work 9 rows in moss (seed) stitch. Change to col 1.

Row 67: Knit.

Rows 68-74: 7 rows in moss (seed) stitch.

Making up

Cast (bind) off purlwise. Darn in ends.

Place Mat 2: Colour Variation 2

Using col 2, cast (bind) on 57 sts.

Rows 1-12: Work 12 rows in moss (seed) stitch. Change to col 3.

Row 13: Knit.

Rows 14-24: Work 11 rows in moss (seed) stitch. Change to col 1.

Row 25: Knit.

Rows 26-36: Work 11 rows in moss (seed) stitch. Change to col 2.

Row 37: Knit.

Rows 38-46: Work 9 rows in moss (seed) stitch. Change to col 3.

Row 47: Knit.

Rows 48-56: Work 9 rows in moss (seed) stitch. Change to col 1.

Row 57: Knit.

Rows 58-66: Work 9 rows in moss (seed) stitch. Change to col 2.

Row 67: Knit.

Rows 68-74: 7 rows in moss (seed) stitch.

Making up

Cast (bind) off purlwise. Darn in ends.

Strap

Make one per table mat

If you wish to make a strap with button hole, you can find the technique needed on page 82.

Using col 3, cast (bind) on 35 sts.

Row 1 (WS): Purl.

Row 2: K3, yo (to create a stitch, which becomes the buttonhole), then k2tog, K to end.

Cast (bind) off.

Making up

Darn in ends.

For each mat: Roll up your table mat and place the strap around the mat to position the button. Stitch the button in place and fasten the strap around the mat

Note: If desired, pin out your table mat onto a flat surface to straighten the sides then spray with cold water. Leave to dry completely.

Simple increases

Not all knitting is worked straight; for garments and some other projects you will need to increase the number of stitches you work

I n order to change the shape of your knitting, you'll need to increase and decrease the number of stitches that you work. Here we will focus on increasing (inc) stitches. There are many ways to increase stitches, and some are more decorative than others. We will show you some of the most common ways to increase the number of stitches that you work. Once you become more experienced in knitting techniques, you'll be able to understand the directions on patterns that instruct you to increase in alternative ways.

Most increases add one or two stitches at a time, and usually at the end of rows. In order to keep a neat selvedge, you will usually perform an increase one stitch in. You'll notice that the shaping will travel diagonally, and sometimes the increase stitch will form part of the design.

If you have to work increases on multiple rows, it's a good idea to keep a notebook and pen to hand; this way you can note down how many increases you have worked either by tally charts or any other method that will help you remember. You'll find this particularly helpful if you have to leave your knitting at some point.

TOP TIP

If you have to make several increases across the row for a designated number of rows, use stitch markers on your needle so that the increase positions are easily seen.

Knit into front and back of stitch (kfb)

When you work this increase, it forms a bar effect, giving it the alternative name of bar increase

01 Knit the stitch
Knit (K) the next stitch, but don't drop the working loop off the left-hand needle. Insert the tip of the right needle into the back of the loop on the left needle.

02 Wind the yarn
Wind the yarn around the tip of the right needle as if working a knit stitch (K), catch the yarn and pull it through the loop, dropping the stitch off the left needle.

03 Continue
You have now created an extra stitch. Continue to work the rest of the row as instructed in your pattern.

Purl into front and back of stitch (pfb)

Increasing on a purl row is rare, but there may be occasions when you need to do so

01 Purl the next stitch
Purl (P) the next stitch, but don't drop the working loop off the left-hand needle. Insert the tip of the right needle into the back of the loop on the left needle from left to right.

02 Wind the yarn
Wind the yarn around the tip of the right needle as if working a purl stitch, catch the yarn and pull it through the loop, dropping the stitch off the left needle.

03 Continue
You have now created an extra stitch. Continue to work the rest of the row as instructed in your pattern.

Make 1 Knitwise (M1 or M1K)

Favoured for increases in the middle of a row, as it's almost invisible

01 Knit to increase
Knit (K) to the point in the pattern that instructs you to increase (inc). Guide the tip of the left needle and insert it under the horizontal strand between the previous and next stitch.

02 Wind the yarn
Insert the tip of the right needle into the back of the raised strand, wind yarn around needle tip as if to knit (K) the stitch, and draw the yarn through.

03 Drop the loop
Drop the loop from the left needle. You have now 'made' another stitch. If you didn't work into the back of the loop, you would create a hole in your work.

Make 1 Purlwise (M1 or M1P)

Perfect for toy making and increasing in the middle of a row

01 Work to increase

Work to the point in the pattern that instructs you to increase. Guide the tip of the left needle and insert it from front to back under the horizontal strand between the previous and next stitch.

02 Wind the yarn

Insert the tip of the right needle into the back of the raised strand from left to right, wind the yarn around the needle tip as if to purl the stitch, and draw the yarn through.

03 Drop the loop

Drop the loop from the left needle. You have now 'made' another stitch. If you didn't work into the back of the loop, you would create a hole in your work.

Simple purse

It's now time to put everything you've learned into practice and make a simple but attractive purse to carry your coins

Difficulty ★★☆☆☆

Skills needed

Increasing
Decreasing (see page 40)
Knitting in rows
Seaming

Finished measurements

Purse measures approx 12.5cm (5in) at widest part x 8cm (3¼in) measured laid flat.

Yarn

For this project you will need a DK yarn. In this example we have used Patons Diploma Gold DK in Violet. You will need one ball of your chosen yarn.

Tension (Gauge)

22st and 30 rows = 10cm (4in) in st st using 4mm needles — tension is not critical for this project.

Needles

4mm (US 6) needles

Other supplies

Tapestry needle
2 press studs (poppers)

Did you know?

Early knitting needles were crafted out of bone, ivory, wood and even tortoise shell!

"If you didn't work into the back of the loop, you would create a hole in your work"

Simple purse

Cast (bind) on 20 sts.

Knit 3 rows.

Start increases

Row 1 (RS): K2, kfb, K to last 3 sts kfb, K2.

Row 2: K2, P to last 2 sts, K2.

Rep these 2 rows until you have 30 sts.

Next row: Knit.

Next row: K2, P to last 2 sts, K2 (28 sts).

Rep last 2 rows 4 more times.

Create fold

Next row (RS): Purl.

Next row (WS): Knit.

Next row: Knit.

Next row: K2, P to last 2 sts, K2.

Rep last 2 rows 4 more times.

Start decreases

Row 1: K2, ssk, K to last 3 sts k2tog, K2.

Row 2: K2, P to last 2 sts, K2.

Hep last 2 rows until 20 sts rem.

Work Row 1 again.

Create flap fold

Next row (WS): Knit.

Flap

Row 1: K2, ssk, K to last 3 sts k2tog, K2 (18 sts).

Row 2: K2, P to last 2 sts, K2.

Rep these 2 rows until 10 sts rem.

Knit 2 rows.

Cast (bind) off knitwise.

Making up

Darn in the ends and block them with a hot iron and damp tea towel with the wrong side facing up, being careful not to press the garter stitch edges.

With right sides facing, join the sides of the purse. Sew on the press studs to the corners of the underside of the flap and corresponding places on the body of the purse.

Decorative increases

The stitches used here may also be used to create decorative effects, for example in ripple stitch techniques (page 40) or in lace garments (page 44). When a variety of increase and decrease methods are worked together the results can be beautiful and intricate. Don't shy away from these types of patterns; you have mastered knit and purl, and they are your foundations to make anything.

Simple decreases

Use these simple stitches to shape your work or pair them with increases to create texture and lace patterns

If you're creating a garment that needs to get smaller as it goes along, for example a hat, then you will need to use decreases (dec) to reduce the number of stitches on your needles, and therefore the size of your piece. Decreases can also be used together with increases (inc) to add decorative elements to your work. Knitting or purling two stitches together (k2tog or p2tog) is one of the simplest decreases, and will cause your work to lean to the right. In order to make your work lean to the left, you will need to use a different decrease (see slip slip knit (ssk) on page 49). These decreases can be used together to create interesting shapes and textures in your work. These stitches can also be adapted to decrease by more than one stitch at a time by knitting/purling more than two together at a time.

Knit two together (k2tog)
Check out the knitting way

01 Needle through two
Insert the right-hand needle through the second and then the first stitch on the right needle, from left to right, as if to knit.

02 Make a new stitch
Knit (K) into the two stitches by wrapping the working yarn around the tip of the right-hand needle, then pull it through both loops to create the new stitch. Drop both of the old stitches off the left-hand needle

03 Slant to the right
Your stitch count will now be reduced by one, because two stitches have been turned into one. You will see that your decrease (dec) slants to the right.

Purl two together (p2tog)
Now try the purling way

01 Needle through two
Insert the right-hand needle through the first and then the second stitch on the right needle, from right to left, as if to purl.

02 Make a new stitch
Purl (P) into the two stitches by wrapping the working yarn around the tip of the right-hand needle, then pull it through both loops to create the new stitch. Drop both of the old stitches off the left-hand needle

03 Slant to the right
Your stitch count will be reduced by one as you've joined two together. You will see that your decrease (dec) slants to the right.

Bobbles tea cosy

It's undoubtedly one of the most rewarding items to knit! Learn how to make the perfect tea cosy, ready to keep your hot drinks hot

Difficulty ★★★☆☆

Skills needed

Decreasing
Knitting in rows
Bobbles
Seaming
Pompom

Finished measurements

23cmx21cm (9x8in) laid flat

Yarn

For this project you will require an Aran weight yarn. In the shown example, Drops Alaska and Drops Nepal were used. The Alaska is 100% wool, while the Nepal is 65% wool and 35% alpaca.

Colour 1: Off White; 2 x balls
Colour 2: Grey Pink; 1 x ball
Colour 3: Goldenrod; 1 x ball
Colour 4: Light Olive; 1 x ball
Colour 5: Cerise; 1 x ball

Tension (Gauge)

18 sts and 24 rows = 10cm (4in) in stocking stitch

Needles

5mm (US 8) needles

Other supplies

Tapestry needle

Pattern notes

To make the bobbles:
K into front, back and front of next st, turn and K3, turn and P3, turn and K3, turn and sl1, k2tog, psso.
On the sample, 16 bobbles in four different colours are worked on each side.

Bobbles tea cosy

Make 2 pieces.
With col 1, cast (bind) on 45 sts.
Knit 4 rows.
Starting with a purl row, work in stocking

stitch until work measures 13cm (5in), adding bobbles in multiple colours randomly, working bobbles on any knit row.

Top shaping

Continuing to add bobbles on knit rows, shape as follows, starting with a knit row.
Row 1 (dec): K7, k2tog *K6, k2tog * work from * to * to last 4 sts, K4 — 40 sts.
Row 2 and every following alternate row: Purl.
Row 3 (dec): K6, k2tog, *K5, k2tog*, work from * to * to last 4 sts, K4 — 35 sts.
Row 5 (dec): K5, k2tog, *K4, k2tog*, work from * to * to last 4 sts, K4 — 30 sts.
Row 7 (dec): K4, k2tog, *K3, k2tog*, work

from * to * to last 4 sts, K4 — 25 sts.
Row 9 (dec): K3, k2tog, *K2, k2tog, work from * to * to end — 19 sts.
Row 11 (dec): K2, k2tog, *K1, k2tog,* work from * to * to end — 13 sts.
Row 13 (dec): K2tog to last st, K1 — 7 sts.
Row 15 (dec): Cast off remaining sts.
Rep for second piece.
Press edges under a damp cloth.
Pin onto teapot to mark where gaps for handle and spout need to be. Sew up seams, leaving gaps for handle and spout.

Pompom

Using col 2, make pompom. Trim and sew onto top centre, secure.

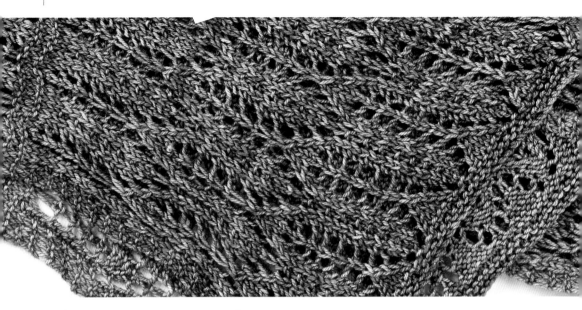

Yarn-over increases

A more decorative method than practical increases, yarn overs add stitches, but also create a hole

Common in lace work and often used for making eyelets, a yarn-over increase is made by looping the yarn around the right-hand needle before making the next stitch. It is important that the loop is wrapped around the needle in the correct way or it will become crossed when worked in the next row, which closes the hole. Yarn overs are normally worked in between two stitches as opposed to at the beginning or end of a row in order to create decorative holes and gaps in the knit.

TOP TIP

As yarn-over increases are mostly used to add decorative holes to knitting, they will often be paired with a decrease. Pair a double yarn over with a k2tog before the increase and a ssk immediately after for a pretty flower bud effect.

Yarn over between knit stitches
Add decorative holes

01 Bring the yarn over
In between two stitches, bring the yarn forward (yf) and wrap it over the top of the right-hand needle. Then work the next knit stitch in the usual way.

02 Check stitch
When you have completed the knit stitch, you will see that the yarn-over increase (yo) is correctly formed on the right-hand needle with the right leg of the loop in front

03 Purl as usual
When you reach the yarn over (yo) on the next row, purl it through the front of the loop in the usual way. This will ensure it creates the open stitch below.

Yarn over between purl stitches
Make decorative holes between purl stitches

01 Bring the yarn over
In between two stitches, bring the yarn backwards and wrap it over the top of the right-hand needle. Work the next stitch as usual.

02 Check stitch
When you have completed the purl stitch, you will see that the yarn-over increase (yo) is correctly formed on the right-hand needle with the right leg of the loop in front.

03 Knit as usual
When you reach the yarn over (yo) on the next row, knit it through the front of the loop in the usual way. This will ensure it creates the open stitch below.

Double yarn over
A bigger hole, great for buttonholes

01 Bring the yarn over twice
In between two knit stitches, bring the yarn forward (yf) and wrap it over the top of the right-hand needle. Then bring it to the front between the needles and wrap it over the top of the right-hand needle again.

02 Knit the next stitch
With the yarn in the back, knit the next stitch in the usual way. This creates two new loops on the right-hand needle.

03 Purl then knit
When you reach the yarn overs on the next row (a purl row), purl the first and then knit the second. This creates a bigger hole than a single yarn over that is great for buttonholes.

Simple lace scarf

Combine the increase and decrease techniques to create a feminine and pretty lace scarf

Difficulty ★★★☆☆

Skills needed

Increasing
Decreasing
Lace
Knitting in rows
Working from a chart or written directions

Finished measurements

Approximately 22x160cm (9x63in)

Yarn

For this project you will need a 3-ply yarn. In the example, Malabrigo Sock yarn was used, it is 100% wool. It uses the Aguas shade. You will need a total of 402m (440yd).

Tension (Gauge)

25 sts and 26 rows = 10cm (4in) in Lace Pattern 2

Needles

4mm (US 6) needles

Other supplies

2 removable stitch markers
Tapestry needle

Notes

If you find charts difficult to work with, don't despair. Many designers usually provide written versions of stitch patterns for those knitters who prefer to use them. If not, it is very easy to create your own. All you need to do is write down the stitches in each row, remembering to read right side (RS) rows from right to left and wrong side (WS) rows from left to right.

Note: Find out how to read stitch symbol charts by turning to page 151.

Janine Le Cras

Janine is a lifelong knitter who learned to knit at her grandmother's knee. After a break she discovered the world of knitting on the web, which had a new and vibrant image, and was re-inspired to pick up her needles.

Simple lace scarf

Cast (bind) on 55 sts.

Knit 4 rows.

Next row: K3, PM, following the chart or written instructions, work Lace Pattern 1, working the sts enclosed by the red lines 6 times in total, PM, K3.

Note: The markers are there to remind you that the three stitches at either edge are to be worked in garter stitch as a border. Garter stitch is great for borders on scarves and shawls as it prevents the edges of the work from curling in.

You might want to add more markers in different colours from the edging markers between each repeat of the lace pattern across your scarf to help you keep track of where you are in the pattern. To do this, add a marker to your needle between every set of 8 stitches (not including the edging stitches).

Continue following the chart or written directions for Lace Pattern 1, using the key to identify the different stitches used, until you have completed all 16 rows shown. Then repeat those 16 rows a further 2 times.

Knit 4 rows.

Next row: K3, sm, following the chart or written instructions, work Lace Pattern 2, working the sts enclosed by the red lines 6 times in total, sm, K3.

Note: If you used extra stitch markers to divide up your repeats of the lace pattern, you need to remove these and reposition them as Lace Pattern 2 has a different number of stitches in each repeat than Lace Pattern 1. Lace Pattern 2 has 6 stitches in a repeat, so you need to place a stitch marker between each set of 6 stitches (not including the edging stitches). Note that on the chart there is a single stitch after the border sts, but before the first pattern repeat, so you might want to place a stitch marker after that stitch to remind you where your first pattern repeat begins.

Continue following the chart or written directions for Lace Pattern 2 until you have completed all 12 rows of the chart. Then repeat those 12 rows a further 21 times.

Knit 4 rows.

Next row: K3, sm, following chart or written instructions, work Lace Pattern 3, working the sts enclosed by the red lines 8 times in total, sm, K3.

Note: If you are using the optional stitch markers, you need to move them to 8-stitch intervals as for the first chart.

Continue following the chart or written directions for Lace Pattern 3 until you have completed all 16 rows of the chart. Then repeat those 16 rows a further 2 times.

Knit 4 rows.

Cast (bind) off.

Making up

Lace always needs to be blocked to bring out its best qualities. Simply soak the scarf in water with a little wool wash added, rinse it, and squeeze out as much water as possible. Wrapping it in a towel and then treading all over it is a pretty good way to get the most water out of it once you have squeezed out as much as you can by hand. Don't wring your knitting, just squeeze it firmly. You don't want to felt it!

Once you have removed as much water as possible, pin out the scarf to the dimensions given in the pattern on a soft surface such as blocking mats. If you don't have blocking mats, a carpet or a spare bed works just as well.

As you pin out the scarf, you will see that the lace opens out so that you can see the pattern created by all those decreases and yarn overs.

Try to keep the edges of the scarf straight either by using blocking wires threaded through or lots of pins short distances apart so as not to make scalloped edges down the sides.

Leave the scarf pinned out until it is completely dry, then unpin, sew in any ends and wear with pride!

Lace pattern 1

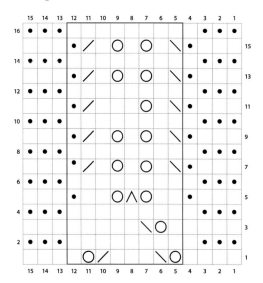

Written Versions of the Lace Patterns

Row 1 (RS): K3, sm, K1, (yo, ssk, K3, k 2tog, yo, K1), work sts in brackets 6 times in all, sm, K3.

Row 2 (WS): K3, sm, P to last 3 sts, sm, K3.

Row 3 (RS): K3, sm, K1, (K1, yo, ssk, K1, k2tog, yo, K2), work sts in brackets 6 times in all, sm, K3.

Row 4 (WS): K3, sm, P to last 3 sts, sm, K3.

Row 5 (RS): K3, sm, P1, (K2, yo, sl1, k2tog, psso, yo, K2, P1), work sts in brackets 6 times in all, sm, K3.

Row 6 (WS): K3, sm, P to last 3 sts, sm, K3.

Row 7 (RS): K3, sm, P1, (ssk, [K1, yo] 2 times, K1, k2tog, P1), work sts in brackets 6 times in all, sm, K3.

Row 8 (WS): K3, sm, P to last 3 sts, sm, K3.

Row 9 (RS): K3, sm, P1, (ssk, [K1, yo] 2 times, K1, k2tog, P1), work sts in brackets 6 times in all, sm, K3.

Row 10 (WS): K3, sm, P to last 3 sts, sm, K3.

Row 11 (RS): K3, sm, P1, (ssk, [K1, yo] 2 times, K1, k2tog, P1), work sts in brackets 6 times in all, sm, K3.

Row 12 (WS): K3, sm, P to last 3 sts, sm, K3.

Row 13 (RS): K3, sm, P1, (ssk, [K1, yo] 2 times, K1, k2tog, P1), work sts in brackets 6 times in all, sm, K3.

Row 14 (WS): K3, sm, P to last 3 sts, sm, K3.

Row 15 (RS): K3, sm, P1, (ssk, [K1, yo] 2 times, K1, k2tog, P1), work sts in brackets 6 times in all, sm, K3.

Row 16 (WS): K3, sm, P to last 3 sts, sm, K3.

Lace pattern 2

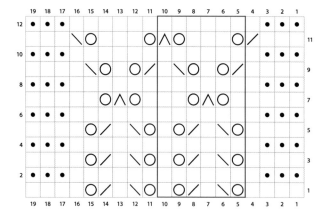

Written Versions of the Lace Patterns

Row 1 (RS): K3, sm, K1 (yo, ssk, K1, k2tog, yo, K1), work sts in brackets 8 times in all, sm, K3.

Row 2 (WS): K3, sm, P to last 3 sts, sm, K3.

Row 3 (RS): K3, sm, K1 (yo, ssk, K1, k2tog, yo, K1), work sts in brackets 8 times in all, sm, K3.

Row 4 (WS): K3, sm, P to last 3 sts, sm, K3.

Row 5 (RS): K3, sm, K1 (yo, ssk, K1, k2tog, yo, K1), work sts in brackets 8 times in all, sm, K3.

Row 6 (WS): K3, sm, P to last 3 sts, sm, K3.

Row 7 (RS): K3, sm, K1, (K1, yo, sl1, k2tog, psso, yo, K2), work sts in brackets 8 times in all, sm, K3.

Row 8 (WS): K3, sm, P to last 3 sts, sm, K3.

Row 9 (RS): K3, sm, K1, (k2tog, yo, K1, yo, ssk, K1), work sts in brackets 8 times in all, sm, K3.

Row 10 (WS): K3, sm, P to last 3 sts, sm, K3.

Row 11 (RS): K3, sm, K1, (yo, K3, yo, sl1, k2tog, psso), work sts in brackets 8 times in all, sm, K3.

Row 12 (WS): K3, sm, P to last 3 sts, sm, K3.

Lace pattern 3

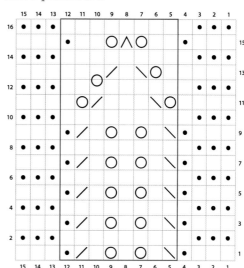

Written Versions of the Lace Patterns

Row 1 (RS): K3, sm, P1, (ssk, [K1, yo] 2 times, K1, k2tog, P1), work sts in brackets 6 times in all, sm, K3.

Row 2 (WS): K3, sm, P to last 3 sts, sm, K3.

Row 3 (RS): K3, sm, P1, (ssk, [K1, yo] 2 times, K1, k2tog, P1), work sts in brackets 6 times in all, sm, K3.

Row 4 (WS): K3, sm, P to last 3 sts, sm, K3.

Row 5 (RS): K3, sm, P1, (ssk, [K1, yo] 2 times, K1, k2tog, P1), work sts in brackets 6 times in all, sm, K3.

Row 6 (WS): K3, sm, P to last 3 sts, sm, K3.

Row 7 (RS): K3, sm, P1, (ssk, [K1, yo] 2 times, K1, k2tog, P1), work sts in brackets 6 times in all, sm, K3.

Row 8 (WS): K3, sm, P to last 3 sts, sm, K3.

Row 9 (RS): K3, sm, P1, (ssk, [K1, yo] 2 times, K1, k2tog, P1), work sts in brackets 6 times in all, sm, K3.

Row 10 (WS): K3, sm, P to last 3 sts, sm, K3.

Row 11 (RS): K3, sm, K1, (yo, ssk, K3, k2tog, yo, K1), work sts in brackets 6 times in all, sm, K3.

Row 12 (WS): K3, sm, P to last 3 sts, sm, K3.

Row 13 (RS): K3, sm, K1, (K1, yo, ssk, K1, k2tog, yo, K2), work sts in brackets 6 times in all, sm, K3.

Row 14 (WS): K3, sm, P to last 3 sts, sm, K3.

Row 15 (RS): K3, sm, P1, (K2, yo, sl1, k2tog, psso, yo, K2, P1), work sts in brackets 6 times in all, sm, K3.

Row 16 (WS): K3, sm, P to last 3 sts, sm, K3.

Key:

RS: knit **WS:** purl	**RS:** yo **WS:** yo	**RS:** k2tog **WS:** p2tog
Pattern repeat		
RS: purl **WS:** knit	**RS:** ssk **WS:** p2tog tbl	**RS:** sl1, k2tog, psso **WS:** sl1 wyif, p2tog tbl, psso

Textural decreases

Use these decreases in order to add texture and direction to your shaped knitting

TOP TIP

Placing a stitch marker on your needle at the point where you need to decrease, if you are carrying out decreases on multiple rows will help you keep your place.

In the same way that patterns call for stitches to be increased (inc), you will sometimes need to decrease (dec) the number of stitches you work in order to create different shapes. The guides on page 40 have already explained the basic decreases of knit two stitches together (k2tog), and purl two stitches together (p2tog), and while these are the most commonly used, the four decreases on this page can offer a more subtle decorative stitch to your knitting. For example, slip, slip, knit (ssk) is a common decrease on sock designs to ensure that the stitches on one side of the toe slant in the right direction. Also see the bunting pattern on page 108, ssk is used on right side of the triangle to follow the contour of the shape to the bottom point, it is coupled with k2tog ,which slants to the right on the other end of the row. A variety of decrease stitches are also used in lacework patterns, usually just before or just after a yarn-over increase to create pretty textural patterns.

"A variety of decrease stitches are also used in lacework to create pretty textural patterns"

Slip 1, knit 1, pass slipped stitch over (sl1, K1, psso)
This decrease stitch will slant to the left of your knitting, so is worked on the right edge

01 Drop a stitch
Insert the tip of the right needle into the next stitch on the left needle as if to knit it, but instead slip it off the left needle without working it, then knit the next stitch.

02 Pick up the stitch
With the tip of the left needle, insert it from left to right into the front of the slipped stitch.

03 Lift it up and over
Lift the slipped stitch up and over the knitted stitch, in much the same way as you would do for casting off. You have now passed the slipped stitch over the knitted stitch and decreased the number of stitches by one.

Slip, slip, knit (ssk)
Often used in sock design

01 Slip it without working

Insert the tip of the right needle into the next stitch on the left needle as if to knit it, but instead slip it off the left needle without working it. Repeat for the next stitch.

02 Knit them together

Guide the tip of the left needle into the front loops of the two slipped stitches. Wind the yarn anticlockwise around the tip of the right needle and knit the stitches together.

03 Decrease

You have now decreased by one stitch, notice how it slants to the left; this decrease is often used on the right hand edge of knitted pieces.

Slip, slip, purl (ssp)
Not commonly used for decreases, usually used in lace

01 Slip two stitches

Slip the next two stitches, individually, knitwise (insert needle as if to knit the stitch, but without working slip it from left to right needle). Insert the left needle into the front loops of both the slipped stitches and transfer them back to the left needle.

02 Pick up both stitches

With the right needle at the back of the work, insert it first from left to right into the second stitch, then into first stitch. Bring right-hand needle tip to the front of work.

03 Slip them off

Wrap yarn anticlockwise around tip of right needle as if to purl, then draw yarn through both loops and slip them off the left needle.

Double decreases
Learn how to decrease two stitches at once

01 Knit three stitches together (k3tog)

This is essentially the same as k2tog. Guide the tip of the right needle into the left side of the third stitch on the left needle, then push it through the second and first stitch. Wind yarn around needle and knit the three stitches together. Two stitches have been decreased.

02 Double slip decrease (sk2p)

Slip the next stitch knitwise from left to right needle, knit the next two stitches together, then using the tip of the left needle, insert it into the slipped stitch and lift it over the worked stitch and off the needle.

03 Slip 2, K1, pass slipped stitch over (s2 K1 psso)

Insert the right needle into the first 2 stitches on the left needle as if to k2tog, but slip them off onto the right needle, K1, then insert the left needle into the two slipped stitches from left to right and lift them over the worked stitch and off the needle

Working on double-pointed needles

Double-pointed needles (DPNs) are used to knit a tubular shape such as socks, and are often used to make the yokes of jumpers

For centuries people have been knitting socks and stockings, and history books suggest that most of this knitting was done on double-pointed needles (DPNs). Whole villages of women, men and children were part of the sock knitting industry until the dawn of mechanisation and knitting machines made the process faster and cheaper.

Now, though, sock knitting has become popular again, and while they can be made on a circular needle, they're just as easy to knit on four or five double-pointed needles. While the prospect of knitting with more than two needles can be daunting, when you actually get started you'll see that the process makes perfect sense. All you are doing is transferring the stitches of one needle to an empty needle, knitting around and around in a spiral.

Socks are knit on short double-pointed needles (DPNs), but longer ones are available, and these can be used to work jumpers in the round, up to the armholes. The sleeves are then worked separately, in the round, then the yoke and neck can be worked in the round. This is the perfect way to knit for those who dislike seaming.

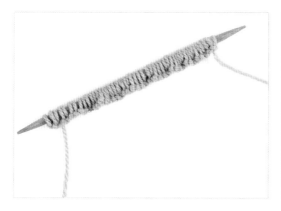

01 Cast (bind) on stitches

Cast (bind) on the number of stitches as specified in your pattern. If you're starting with a rib, you need a nice stretchy cast (bind) on such as the long tail cast (bind) on (page 18).

02 Arrange stitches

Evenly distribute the cast (bind) on stitches across 3 or 4 needles — most sock patterns suggest 3 needles but either way you will work in the same way. Place the needles on a flat surface and arrange as illustrated with the working tail of yarn on the right and all cast (bind) on loops facing inwards. Ensure that there is no twist between the needles, as this will show when you knit your first round.

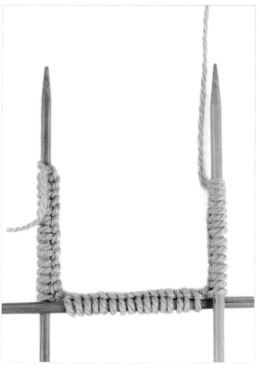

TOP TIP

If the stitches become crowded on one needle, use needle stops to prevent stitches falling off or add in a double-pointed needle (DPN) and redistribute the stitches.

03 Join the round

Slip the first stitch off the left needle, onto the right needle to meet your last cast (bind) on stitch. Now insert the tip of the left needle into the last cast (bind) on stitch and slip it over the stitch you just slipped and onto the left needle. Now you are ready to work. With your fourth needle, start to knit in the round. As you are working in the round, it is difficult to see the beginning and end of each round, so place a stitch marker between the first and second stitch.

Tension (gauge)

When changing needles it is essential to keep an even tension (gauge). If the stitches are too loose at the needle junction, a ladder will appear in your knitting. To avoid this, start knitting with the new needle on top of the old, and pull the first stitch tight.

Picot-topped ankle socks

Learn how to make this pretty project using the below pattern and achieve a decoratively topped sock you can be proud of

Difficulty ★★★★☆

Skills needed
Decreasing
Lace stitches
Pick up & knit
Knitting in rounds
Seaming
Turning a heel

Finished measurements
The pattern is designed to fit a women's UK size 6 (US size 8) of average width, but the length can be adjusted — see notes in the pattern.

Yarn
For this pattern you will need a 4-ply yarn. For the example, Rowan Fine Art yarn was used in Rowan. You will need roughly 250m (275yd).

Tension (Gauge)
30 stitches and 38 rounds = 10cm (4in) in stocking (stockinette) stitch (st st)

Needles
2.75mm (US 2) 5x double-pointed needles (DPNs)

Other supplies
1 stitch marker
Tapestry needle

Construction notes
Both socks are worked in the same way

Picot-topped ankle socks

Cast (bind) 60 sts.

Arrange over 4 needles as follows:
Needles 1 & 3: 16 sts.
Needles 2 & 4: 14 sts, being careful not to twist the stitches.
Slip the first stitch on the LH needle onto the RH needle, then pass the first stitch on the RH needle over the top of the stitch you just slipped and place it on the LH needle. This will be the first stitch you work.

Place a stitch marker between stitches 1 and 2 to denote the beginning of the round.
Rnd 1: (K1, P1) to end of rnd.
Rep Rnd 1 3 more times.
Next rnd: (K2tog, yo) to end of rnd. This will create the pretty picot edge around the top of the sock.
Rep round 1 4 more times.
Knit 8 rounds.
Next rnd: (K2, k2tog, yo) to end of rnd.
Knit 4 rounds.
Next rnd: (k2tog, yo, K2) to end of rnd.
Knit 8 rounds

Note: For a longer sock cuff, add more knit rounds here.

Divide for heel

Knit the first 30 sts on to one needle, leaving the rem sts on 2 spare needles.

Turn and working in rows on the first 30 sts, work as follows:
How 1: Sl1, P to end.
Row 2: Sl1, K to end.
Repeat these 2 rows 8 times more. Then work Row 1 again.

Turn heel

Row 1 (RS): Sl1, K16, ssk, K1. Turn work.
Row 2 (WS): Sl1, P5, p2tog, P1. Turn work.
Row 3 (RS): Sl1, K6, ssk, K1. Turn work.
Row 4 (WS): Sl1, P7, p2tog, P1. Turn work.
Cont in this way, working 1 more st each row before dec until 18 sts remain.
Next row: Sl1, K to last 2 sts, ssk.
Next row: Sl 1, P to last 2 sts, p2tog. (16 sts)

Gusset

With RS facing, K8 sts onto one needle.
Needle 1 (next needle): K next 8 sts, then pick up and K 10 sts down side of heel.
Needle 2: Knit across 30 sts that were held on spare needles.
Needle 3: Pick up and K10 sts up side of heel flap, then K the 8 sts on the first needle.
Continue as follows:
Rnd 1:
Needle 1 (dec): K to last 3 sts, k2tog, K1.
Needle 2: K all sts.
Needle 3 (dec): K1, ssk, K to end of needle.
Rnd 2: Knit all sts.
Rep last 2 rnds until:
Needle 1: 15 sts rem.
Needle 2: 30 sts.
Needle 3: 15 sts rem.
Now knit every round until work, from heel to needles, measures 20cm (8in).

Note: Alternatively, to work a shorter or longer foot, measure the wearer's foot from the back of the heel to the base of the big toe.
Use this measurement in place of the measurement above.

Shape toe

Rnd 1:
Needle 1 (dec): K to last 3 sts, k2tog, K1.
Needle 2 (dec): K1, ssk, K to last 3 sts, k2tog, K1.
Needle 3 (dec): K1, ssk, K to end of needle.
Rnd 2: Knit all sts.
Rep last 2 rounds until 40 sts rem.
Rep round 1 until 24 sts rem.
Place stitches from needles 1 and 3 onto one needle. With RS facing, graft the toe using kitchener stitch.

Making up

Darn in ends. Turn sock inside out, and fold the cuff over so that the cast (bind)-on edge is in line with the last row of rib stitching. You will now see that the picot edge is visible. With needle and yarn, join the cast (bind)-off edge to the body of the sock, along the line of the last rib round.

Knitting in the round

Using a circular needle to work garments in the round, means that you won't need to sew up as many seams

W e've already looked at knitting in the round using 4 double-pointed needles on page 50, but if you find that method a bit too fiddly, try knitting with a circular needle. Working in this way, you will create a tube of knitting, and because the work is never turned, the right side is always facing you. To create a stocking stitch finish, simply knit every round. For a garter stitch, alternate rounds of knit and purl.

Working in the round is the perfect way to knit for those who don't like to join seams. Circular needles come in a variety of lengths, making them ideal to knit an array of garments from socks to cowls and full-sized sweaters. If you do plan to knit a sweater on a circular needle, be aware that the weight of the garment can be quite cumbersome and heavy, although when working a lot of stitches, most of their weight is distributed on the cable, which is easier on the hands and wrists compared to working the same number of stitches on straight needles.

TOP TIP

If the pattern requires shaping via increases and decreases, use stitch markers of a different colour to show where these actions need to take place on the round.

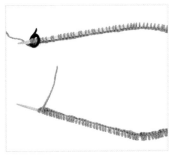

01 Mark the round

Holding the ends of the circular needle in each hand, cast on as you normally would. Once you have cast on the required number of stitches stated in the pattern, slip a stitch marker onto the right-hand needle. This will mark the beginning and end of the round.

02 Join the round

When joining the round, ensure that the stitches haven't twisted around the cable, and all the stitches face into the middle of the cable. When working the first stitch of the first round, pull the yarn with some tension.

03 Work in the round

Continue to work in the round as stated on the pattern. As you are knitting a tube, the right side will always be facing you, and to create a stocking stitch, simply knit every round. Each time you reach the stitch marker, slip it from one needle to the next.

Colourful, cosy cowl

It's now time to practise knitting in the round using a super chunky yarn. This pattern is perfect if you want to knit something cosy, but equally as vibrant and colourful

Difficulty ★★☆☆☆

Skills needed
Simple lace stitches
Knitting in the round

Finished measurements
Circumference: 77.5cm (30.5in)
Height: 23.5cm (9in)

Yarn
For this particular project you will need a super chunky yarn. In this example, Rowan Big Wool colour has been used in the Carnival shade, kindly provided by Rowan. You shall require 160m (174yd).

Tension (Gauge)
9 sts and 12.5 rows = 10x10cm (4x4in) measured over st st using 10mm (US 15) needles, or the size required to obtain the correct tension.

Needles
10mm (US 15) circular needle, 40cm (16in) long.

Other supplies
Stitch marker
Tapestry needle

Colourful, cosy cowl
Using 10mm (US 15) circular needle cast on 70 sts.

Being careful not to twist the cast on stitches, place a stitch marker and join to work in rnds as follows:

Rnd 1: Knit the first row.
Rnd 2: Purl.
Rnd 3: Knit.
Rnd 4: Purl.
Knit 4 rounds.
**Rnd 9:* Purl.
Rnd 10: (yon, k2tog) to end of round.
Rnd 11: Purl.
Knit 4 rounds. **

Rep rnds 9 to 15 twice more.
Rnd 30: Purl.
Rnd 31: Knit.
Rnd 32: Purl.
Cast off kwise (knitting the sts).

Making up
Darn in ends. If you prefer you can block the item but it isn't necessary.

TOP TIP
If you don't have a stitchmarker big enough, cut a 4cm(2in) length of yarn in a contrasting colour, tie into a loose loop and thread onto needle.

Twisted stitches

Often worked in knit stitches on a purl background, cable and twisted stitches offer a raised detail

A dding cables to a piece of knitting is one of the easiest ways to add the 'wow factor' to your work. The technique is worked by displacing a set of stitches onto a cable needle, working the next stitch(es), then working the stitches from the cable needle.

The number of stitches involved and the way they are twisted by holding them in front or behind your work will determine the pattern that can be created. From ropes and plaits, to more complicated Celtic knots, all can be worked to produce the archetypal Aran sweater. Going back 2-300 years, not only were twisted patterns used for decorative purposes, but the thick fabric that these stitches produced combined with wool yarn also created some very warm garments for fishermen to wear on their trawlers.

Currently, twisted and cable stitches are very popular for interior design, featuring on cushions, throws and even replicated in porcelain for vases.

Narrowing fabric

When you knit a piece with cable stitches and twists, be aware that it can have a significant effect on the width of your fabric compared to when the same number of stitches are worked over stocking stitch. Sometimes the length is slightly reduced too. So if you're thinking of adding a column or two of cable pattern to your favourite stocking stitch pattern, work up a swatch first to see what difference it will make to the overall width.

2-stitch twists

An easy way to create a twist without needing a cable needle

Right Twist (T2R)

01 Knit the stitch
Ensuring your yarn is at the back of your work insert the tip of the right-hand needle into the second stitch on the left-hand needle. Work as if to knit the stitch without slipping it off the needle.

02 Work the second stitch
Now knit (K) the second stitch on the needle and pull both loops from the left-hand needle.

03 Crossover stitch
You should see a crossover stitch that slants to the right. While the sample shown is worked on a knit background, you could also work a purl stitch either side of the 2 knit stitches, so that it is even more prominent.

Left Twist (T2L)

01 Position the needles
With your yarn at the back of your knitting, insert the tip of your right needle behind the first stitch on the left needle and into the front of the second stitch.

02 Wind the yarn
Wind the yarn around the tip of the needle and draw through behind the first stitch, without slipping the stitch off the needle.

03 Knit the first stitch
Now knit (K) the first stitch of the left needle and pull both loops from the left needle, you should see that the twist slants to the left.

Cables
Master the basic cabling technique

4 stitch, cable front (C4F)

01 The front
Once you have worked the setup rows, work to the knit stitches for the cable. Slip the next 2 stitches onto the cable needle and leave it at the front of your work.

02 Knit 2 stitches
Now you need to knit the 2 stitches from the left-hand needle.

03 Slide the stitches
Without twisting the cable needle, slide the stitches to the right end of the needle and knit them onto the left needle.

4 stitch, cable back (C4B)

01 The back
Once you have worked the setup rows, work to the knit stitches for the cable. Slip the next 2 stitches onto the cable needle and push it to the back of your work.

02 Knit 2 stitches
Now knit (K) the two stitches from the left-hand needle.

03 Slide the stitches
Without twisting the cable needle, slide the stitches to the right end of the needle and knit them onto the left needle.

Cable jumper tea cosy

Add a little bit of rustic style to tea time with this teapot cosy, a great little project to ease you into using cable stitches. You'll also get to practise decrease and picking up stitches

Difficulty ★★★☆☆

Skills needed

Decreasing
Cables
Pick up and knit
Knitting in rows
Cast (bind) off in rib
Seaming

Finished measurements

To fit a standard 2-pint teapot

Yarn

For this pattern you will need an Aran weight yarn. In this example we have used Sirdar Hayfield Bonus Aran in Ivory Cream. You will need approximately 100m (110yd).

Tension (Gauge)

18 sts and 24 rows = 10cm (4in) in stocking stitch

Needles

5mm (US 8)

Other supplies

Cable needle
Stitch holder
Tapestry needle

TOP TIP

Turn to page 80 to learn how to pick up stitches.

Cable jumper tea cosy
Special st instructions:
C6B: Slip the next 3 stitches onto your cable needle and hold at back of work, knit the next 3 stitches on the left-hand needle, then knit the sts from the cable needle.
Cast (bind) on 60 stitches.
Row 1: (K1, P1) to end of row.
Rep Row 1 3 more times.

Cable pattern starts
Row 1 (RS): *P3, (K6, P3) 3 times, rep from * once more.
Row 2 (WS): *K3, (P6, K3) 3 times, rep from * once more.

Split for handle opening
Row 3 (RS): P3, (K6, P3) 3 times, place the last 30 stitches on a stitch holder, these will be worked later.
** *Row 4 (WS):* K3, (P6, K3) 3 times.
Row 5 (RS): P3, (C6B, P3) 3 times.
Row 6 (WS): As row 4.
Row 7 (RS): P3, (K6, P3) 3 times.
Row 8 (WS): As row 4.
Row 9 (RS): As row 7.
Row 10 (WS): As row 4.
Row 11 (RS): As row 7.
Rep pattern from Row 4 a further 4 times. **

   Cut yarn and place the 30 sts just worked on to a stitch holder.

   Move the stitches from the first stitch holder onto a needle with RS facing. Reattach yarn and work Row 11 above.

   Then work from ** to **. Cut the yarn.

   Place the stitches from the holder onto the needle with RS facing to join the stitches just worked, and work as follows across all 60 stitches.
Row 1 (RS): *P3, (C6B, P3) 3 times, rep from * once more.
Row 2 (WS): *K3, (P6, K3) 3 times, rep from * once more.
Row 3 (RS): *P3, (K6, P3) 3 times, rep from * once more.
Row 4 (WS): As row 2.
Row 5 (RS): As row 3.
Row 6 (WS): As row 2.
Row 7 (RS): As row 3.
Row 8 (WS): As row 2.

Start decreases
Row 1 (dec): *P1, p2tog, (C6B, P1, p2tog) 3 times, rep from * once more — 52 sts.
Row 2: *K2, (P6, K2) 3 times, rep from * once more.
Row 3 (dec): *P2tog, (K4, k2tog, p2tog) 3 times, rep from * once more — 38 sts.
Row 4: *K1, (P5, K1) 3 times, rep from * once more.
Row 5 (dec): *P1, (ssk, K1, k2tog, P1) 3 times, rep from * once more — 26 sts.
Row 6: *K1, (P3, K1) 3 times, rep from * once more.
Row 7 (dec): *P1, (ssk, K1, P1) 3 times, rep from * once more — 20 sts.
Row 8: *K1, (P2, K1) 3 times, rep from * once more.
Row 9 (dec): P1, (k2tog, P1) twice, k2tog, p2tog, (k2tog, P1) 3 times — 13 sts.
Row 10 (dec): P2tog 3 times, K1, p2tog 3 times — 7 sts.
Cut the yarn leaving a long tail. Thread this onto a tapestry needle and insert needle into the 7 remaining stitches. Pull stitches off the needle and draw up tightly. Secure yarn on wrong side of cosy.

Making up
With right sides together, join the sides of the rib section and the first 2 rows of the cable section at the bottom of the cosy. Join the sides along the decrease section at the top of the cosy.

   With the RS the of cosy facing, pick up and knit 20 stitches along one side of one opening.

   Work 4 rows in (K1, P1) rib.

   Cast (bind) off in rib.

   Repeat for other side of the opening. Then repeat on the second opening.

   Darn in all ends.

I-cord

The i-cord is a tubular piece of knitting that is worked using two double-pointed needles (DPNs)

If you're not used to working on double-pointed needles (DPNs), knitting an i-cord can initially seem quite daunting, however, making one is a great introduction to DPNs. While you can make great-looking things for the home, such as the coasters we've made here, i-cords are also perfect for drawstrings and straps for bags, headbands, belts, tie for a hooded top, and more. I-cords look very effective stitched to the edge of a garment in a contrasting colour and can be added in loops to form button holes for toggles.

I-cords are usually worked over between 3 to 6 stitches, on a needle size that fits the weight of the yarn (for example 4mm for DK yarn). They can be worked in one colour, spiralled for a textured finish, and in 2 colours.

Basic i-cord

Learn how to get started with this technique

01 Knit the first row
For a practise i-cord, cast (bind) on 5 stitches using 2 DPNs and knit the first row. *While turning the needle holding the stitches and the bumps to the back, hold it in your left hand and slide the stitches to the other end of the needle.

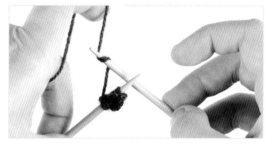

02 Continue knitting
The yarn should be in the back, but on the furthest stitch from the end of the tip of the needle. Taking the empty needle, insert it in the first stitch and with a taut tension pull the yarn and knit the stitch. Knit the other 4 stitches.

03 Even out
Repeating from * in step 1, continue to knit the i-cord to the desired length. Every now and again give the cord a little tug to even out the stitches and rows.

Twisted i-cord

Cast (bind) on 3 stitches and work as for the basic i-cord, but rather than knit every row, alternate between knit and purl stitches, to create a garter stitch effect. This will create an elastic cord.

Striped i-cord

Two simple steps to creating something a bit different

01 Cast (bind) on

Cast (bind) on 5 stitches using yarn shade A and knit the first stitch as normal. Join Yarn shade B then knit the stitch.

02 Start alternating

On the third stitch, swap to yarn A and knit it. Continue to work the i-cord as set in the basic i-cord tutorial, alternating between yarn A and B, working yarn A above yarn A, and yarn B above yarn B stitches.

I-cord coaster

These simple coasters are an easy way of practicing the i-cord technique as well as adding a splash of colour to any surface

Difficulty ★☆☆☆☆

Skills needed
Knitting in rows

Finished measurements
Coaster diameter: 10cm (4in)

Yarn
Oddments of DK yarn. This is a great way to use up yarn left over from other projects

Tension (Gauge)
Tension is not important for this project

Needles
3.5mm (US 4) 2 x DPNs

Other supplies
Tapestry needle

I-cord coaster
Cast (bind) on 4 stitches, leaving a long tail. Following the instructions (page 58), make an i-cord measuring 120cm (47in). Cast (bind) off.

Making up
Starting at the cast (bind) on end of the i-cord, thread the yarn tail onto the tapestry needle. Start to form it into a spiral and start stitching it in place. Gradually spiral and stitch the i-cord until you reach the end. Secure the yarn on the wrong side and tease into a circle shape.

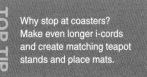

TOP TIP

Why stop at coasters? Make even longer i-cords and create matching teapot stands and place mats.

I-cord cast (bind) off

To try a different way to edge your knitting, work this cast (bind) off in a different colour to add some contrasting detail

O nce Elizabeth Zimmermann had discovered the very easy i-cord (or to give it the full title of Idiot Cord), the technique was adapted and used for a variety of different finishes. Here we'll show you how to complete the i-cord cast (bind) off. Practise on a piece of test knitting first, if you're not confident to work it straight onto your knitting. You work it with your stitches on your main needle and two double-pointed needles (DPNs), which can be tricky at first, but you'll soon find your rhythm.

Unlike a ribbed hem or edge, the i-cord cast (bind) off isn't stretchy or close-fitting, so this is best used for edgings of flat pieces of knitting, or the welt and cuffs of loose fitting garments (such as

the baby jacket on the following pages). Be careful not to pull your stitches too tightly as this can cause puckering of the fabric. While the tutorial below shows you how to cast (bind) off at the end of knitted piece, you could also pick up and knit stitches along the edges of completed pieces, purl (P) 1 row and then work an i-cord cast (bind) off.

Tight tension?
If you find that your tension is a bit too tight and your work is puckering along the cast (bind) off edge, work with a pair of DPNs one size bigger than the needle size you used for the main garment knitting.

I-cord cast (bind) off
End your project with an i-cord

01 Work your pattern
Work the pattern to the cast (bind)-off edge, ending with a knit row. If you are using another colour for the i-cord cast (bind) off, change colours and purl (P) a row. The right side (RS) should be facing you. With the stitches to be cast (bound) off on the needle in your left hand, using the cable cast (bind) on method (see page 17), cast (bind) on 3 stitches at the start of the row with a double-pointed needle (DPN). Knit the first 2 stitches, then separately slip the next 2 stitches knitwise (kwise). Insert the tip of the left needle into the front of the 2 slipped stitches (sl sts) and knit them together. You now have 3 stitches on the right DPN.

02 Work the cast (bind) off
Slide the needle through the stitches so that they are at the other end of the needle, ready to be worked. With the second double-pointed needle (DPN), knit 2 stitches off the first DPN, slip the third stitch knitwise (kwise), then slip the first stitch off the needle holding the stitches to be cast (bound) off. Insert the tip of the left needle into the front of the 2 slipped stitches (sl sts) and knit them together. Repeat this step to the end of the row. You will end up with 3 stitches remaining on the DPN, so cast (bind) these off as normal.

I-cord baby cardigan

Adding an i-cord cast (bind) off to a garment gives it an interesting edge, adding a great finish — perfect for young children's clothes

Difficulty ★★★☆☆

Skills needed

Increasing
Decreasing
Pick up & knit
Knitting in rows
Seaming
I-cord cast (bind) off

Finished measurements

Chest: 48.5 (53.5, 58.5)cm 19 (21, 23)in

Yarn

For this project you will need a DK silk yarn. In the example Rowan Baby Merino DK Silk was used in the colours Snow Drop and Bluebird, kindly provided by Rowan.
Colour 1: Snow drop; 2 (3, 4) x balls
Colour 2: Bluebird; 1 x ball

Tension (Gauge)

21 sts and 30 rows = 10cm (4in) in stocking (stockinette) stitch

Needles

3.5mm (US 4) circular needle
3.5mm 4x double-pointed needles (DPNs)

Other supplies

4 stitch holders
Stitch markers
Tapestry needle
4 buttons of choice

Construction notes

4 stitch holders
Stitch mark

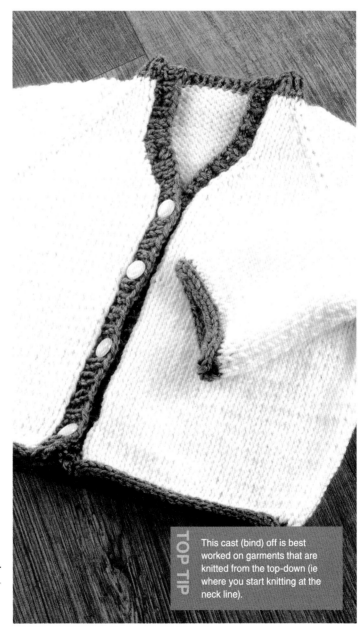

TOP TIP

This cast (bind) off is best worked on garments that are knitted from the top-down (ie where you start knitting at the neck line).

To fit age (months)	0-6	6-12	12-18
Colour 1 (balls)	2	3	4
Colour 2 (balls)	1	1	1

I-cord baby cardigan

Back

Cast (bind) on 32, 36, 46 sts using circular needle and col 2.

Row 1: (K1, P1) to end of row.

Rep row 1 3 more times.

Change to col 1.

Row 1 (RS):

Left Front: K4 (4, 5), place marker.

Left Sleeve: K3, (5, 7), place marker.

Back: K18, (18, 22) place marker.

Right Sleeve: K3, (5, 7), place marker.

Right Front: K4 (4, 5).

Row 2 (WS): Purl.

Start increases

Row 1 (inc): K1, kfb, *K to the last st before the first marker, kfb into this st, slip marker, kfb, rep from * for the rest of the row, then K to last 2 sts, kfb, K1.

Row 2: Purl.

Rep these 2 rows 4 more times — 122 (126, 136) sts.

Neck edge increases

Row 1 (inc): K1, kfb, *K to the last st before the first marker, kfb into this st, slip marker, kfb, rep from * for the rest of the row, then K to last 2 sts, kfb, K1.

Row 2: Purl.

Rep these 2 rows 4 more times — 122 (126, 136) sts.

Cont increases

Row 1 (inc): *K to the last st before the first marker, kfb into this st, slip marker, kfb, rep from * for the rest of the row, then knit to the end of the row.

Row 2: Purl.

Work these 2 rows 6, (8, 9) more times. You should now have a total of: 178 (198, 216) sts on the needle.

This works out as:

Left Front: 26 (28, 30) sts.

Left Sleeve: 37, (43, 47) sts.

Back: 52, (56, 62) sts.

Right Sleeve: 37, (43, 47) sts.

Right Front: 26 (28, 30) sts.

Knit 1 row, Purl 1 row.

Divide for sleeves

On separate holders, place the stitches for the left front, left sleeve, back and right front to work later.

Working on the stitches for the right sleeve continue as follows:

Row 1 (RS): Cast (bind) on 3 sts using the cable method, K to the end of row — 40 (46, 50) sts.

Row 2 (WS): Cast (bind) on 3 sts using the cable method, P to the end of row — 43 (49, 53) sts.

Knit 1 row, Purl 1 row.

Arm decreases

Row 1 (dec): K1, ssk, K to last 3 sts, k2tog, K1.

Row 2: Purl.

Sizes 1 and 2: Rep decrease rows 1 and 2 1 more time — 39 (42) sts.

Sizes 3: Rep decrease rows 1 and 2 2 more times — 47 sts.

Cont in stocking (stockinette) stitch until sleeve is 24 (26.5, 29)cm/9.5 (10.5, 11.5)in from neck edge ending on a K row.

Change to col 2.

Purl 1 row.

Cast (bind) off using the i-cord cast (bind) off.

With right sides (RSs) together join the sleeve seams.

Repeat for left sleeve.

Body

Transfer stitches for left front, back, and right front onto your needle, and with right side facing continue as follows:

Setup row: K across left front and pick up 6 sts along the underside of the left sleeve, K sts for back, pick up 6 sts along the underside of the right sleeve, K across right front — 116 (124, 134) sts.

Work in stocking (stockinette) stitch until back measures 25.5 (28, 30.5)cm/10.5 (11.5, 12.5)in from the cast (bind)-on edge of the neck, ending on a Knit row.

Change to col 2. Purl 1 row.

Cast (bind) off using the i-cord cast (bind) off.

Button band

With right side facing, pick up and K 58 (65, 69) sts along left front edge.

Row 1 (WS): (K1, P1) to end of row.
   Repeat 2 more times. Cast (bind) off in rib.

Buttonhole band

With right side (RS) facing, pick up and Knit 58 (62, 66) sts along right front edge.
Row 1 (WS): (K1, P1) to end of row.
Row 2 (RS, buttonholes): (K1, P1) 7 (9, 7) times, *k2tog, yo, (K1, P1) 4 (4, 5) times, K1, rep from * 3 more times.

Row 3: As row 1.
   Cast (bind) off in rib.

Making up

Darn in all ends. Block gently on reverse of knitting, avoiding rib and i-cord areas.

Did you know?

The i-cord's full title is 'Idiot Cord' named by Elizabeth Zimmermann who accidentally discovered this very simple technique.

Working with two colours

**Over these two pages we will look at Fair Isle knitting and how
to cope with the two different yarns as you knit**

Fair Isle knitting also goes by the names of Jacquard, stranded, two colour and double knitting. Where intarsia knitting is creating an image or shape via stitches in blocks of colour, Fair Isle knitting carries two or more colours along the row on a repeated pattern and is usually worked in stocking (stockinette) stitch.

Due to the stranding/carrying of the yarns at the back of the work, Fair Isle garments tend to be thick and therefore very warm. Because of this it is usual to work these garments in 4ply or DK weight yarns as anything thicker would result in a very bulky piece of clothing.

As you work across the row, you will carry all the yarns with you, alternating between colours as you follow the chart. The yarns need to be stranded (or woven in) as you knit, other wise the loops (floats) on the back can easily get caught on fingers, buttons and other fastenings. You must also be careful not to pull the floats too tightly, otherwise an uneven tension (gauge) and puckered fabric will result.

TOP TIP

If you are adding a Fair Isle pattern chart to your stocking (stockinette) stitch pattern, note that you will need more yarn than originally stated due to the floats being carried.

Fair Isle
Create fetching repeated patterns

01 Work a knit row
With both colour yarns at the back of your work on the knit row, follow the chart and work the stitches in the first colour, then change when necessary by dropping it and picking up the second colour. When you knit the first colour again do not pull it too tightly. So that you don't carry a colour across a large number of stitches, cross it over with the other yarn every third stitch.

02 On a purl row
On a purl row, bring both yarns to the front. Keep the one you are working in your right hand and let the other fall to your left. When you change the yarn over swap their positions.

03 Keep your yarn even
For best results, make sure that your yarn is evenly tensioned (gauged). This will give you a nice flat fabric. At first this may be tricky, but practice, and learning to hold each yarn in a different hand, will ensure great results in no time.

Holding the yarns

If you're keen to improve your Fair Isle skills, try holding the yarns differently

01 Start stitching

When working two colours, hold one yarn in your right hand (RH) as you would normally do, then in a mirror image of your right hand, hold the second colour in your left hand (LH). On a practice piece, work two stitches in yarn from the right hand.

02 Change colours

Now change colours. Insert the tip of the right needle into the next stitch, with the index finger of the left hand guide the second colour to the front of the tip, wind it over the needles and towards the right.

03 Pull it through

Now pull the new stitch through as you would on a regular knit stitch, keeping tension (gauge) on the left yarn.

Hold both yarns in the right hand

If you don't think you can manage two yarns in different hands, hold the first yarn as you usually would over your index finger, then the second yarn on your middle finger.

In the round

When working Fair Isle, it recommended that you work the project in the round on a circular needle or set of double-pointed needles (DPNs). This is so that every round is worked in knit stitch, and you can see the pattern as it grows. Changing and carrying colours on a purl (P) row can be tricky.

Hold both yarns in the left hand

This method is best to use if you prefer to knit the continental way. Hold one yarn on the index finger, and the second yarn on the middle finger of the left hand. When you knit, the technique is more to 'catch' the yarn with your needle, than 'throwing' it around the needle.

How to weave yarn on the wrong side

As you knit, the floats are caught by the yarn on alternate stitches, or every two or three stitches

Weaving in left yarn

With one yarn in each hand, keep the left yarn above the needles when not weaving it in. On both knit and purl rows, lift the float, insert the right needle into the next stitch ready to work it, and under the float. Simply knit or purl as normal under the float and your yarn will be carried.

Weaving in right yarn

This is a little more tricky than weaving the left yarn. When not weaving in, keep the right yarn to the right of the needle tips. Insert the point of the right needle into the next stitch as if to work it and wind the right float around the needle — on a Knit row wind as if to knit, on a Purl row wind the float under then over the needle. Wind the working yarn of the left hand around the needle as normal. Return your right-hand yarn to the normal position, then draw stitch through with the left yarn.

TOP TIP

If you want longer cuffs you can either add a few rounds in the main colour after the chart in knit stitch, or you can have a longer rib by adding rounds.

Fair Isle boot cuffs

Add flair to your plain boots with these Fair Isle boot cuffs. Once you get the hang of working multiple strands of yarn, you'll never want to stop!

Difficulty ★★★★☆

Skills needed
Colourwork (stranded)
Knitting in rounds
Working from a chart

Finished measurements
Size S/M fits calves up to 34cm (13.5in). L fits up too about 40cm (15.75in).
Total length: 13cm (5in)
Width (when laid flat): For S/M: 15cm (6in) and for L 19cm (7.5in)
   As with most knitted accessories the boot cuffs are very stretchy.

Yarn
For this design you will need DK yarn in various colours. In the example shown, Yarn Stories Fine Merino DK has been used in Dove, Raspberry, Primrose, Spring Green, Lilac, Thistle and Leaf.
Colour 1: Dove; 1 x ball
Colour 2: Raspberry; 1 x ball
Colour 3: Primrose; 1 x ball
Colour 4: Spring Green; 1 x ball
Colour 5: Lilac; 1 x ball
Colour 6: Thistle; 1 x ball
Colour 7: Leaf; 1 x ball

Tension (Gauge)
24 sts over 30 rows = 10cm (4in) in Fair Isle pattern using needle 4mm (US 6)

Needles
4mm (US 6) double-pointed needles

Other supplies
2 removable stitch markers
Tapestry needle

Construction notes
There are seven colours at work in the project and that can seem overwhelming. You never use more than two in the same round, so concentrate on that. Cut the main colour yarn when you have finished the upper rib and the first two rounds of the chart. Then you have one less thread getting in your way. Rejoin to knit the final two rounds of the chart and the lower rib.
   The stitches at the beginning/end of the rounds may look untidy. Don't worry as, when you darn in all the ends after knitting, you can always tighten any loose stitches.

Fair Isle boot cuffs
With col 1 and double-pointed needles (DPNs) cast (bind) on 72 (88) sts (18 sts on each needle for S/M, 22 sts on each for L). Join to work in the round and don't twist the cast (bind)-on edge as you do so.
Rnd 1: *K2, P2, rep from * to end.

Next rnd: Work in rib K2, P2.
Continue in K2, p2rib for a further 7 rnds. Work the chart.
Continuing with col 1 and in K2 P2 rib as set previously, work 16 rnds.
   Cast (bind) off loosely in rib.

Making up
Make the other boot cuff the same way.
   Weave in loose ends and block carefully by using an iron set on wool with the steam function on. Wear proudly!

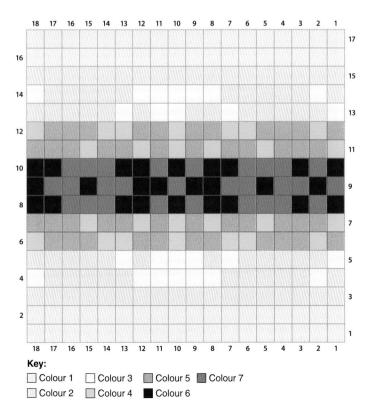

Key:
☐ Colour 1   ☐ Colour 3   ▨ Colour 5   ▨ Colour 7
☐ Colour 2   ☐ Colour 4   ■ Colour 6

Colour work

Adding different colours in horizontal stripes is a fairly easy and simple way to make a plain piece stand out

There are several different ways to add colour to knitting and some are a lot more complicated than others. For example, Fair Isle and intarsia knitting are more advanced techniques that will take a bit of practise and concentration to grasp. However, one fairly easy technique of adding colour is to work in horizontal stripes, which can be added in different sizes and even different fibres to create interesting textures. You can introduce stripes to any single-colour pattern without affecting the tension (gauge) or shape of the knitting. Here are just a few ways to add colour to your knitting. They all have a right side, which is shown in these swatches.

Two-colour garter-stitch stripe

Worked in garter stitch, this stripe pattern uses two colours (A and B) that are alternated every two rows. To work the pattern, knit two rows of A, then two rows of B, and continue until the desired length. When you change colours, drop the yarn not in use at the side of the work and simply pick it up again when needed.

Two-colour knit and purl pinstripe

Working with two colours (A and B), begin by knitting six rows of A in stocking stitch. Then drop A at the side and knit two rows of B. This will create a purl ridge in the second colour on the right side. Repeat this for a pinstripe effect. To avoid loose strands of B at the edge, wrap A around B at the start of every RS row.

Five-colour stocking-stitch stripe

To work stripes in multiple colours and carry the colours up the side of the work, use a circular needle. Work back and forth in rows in stocking stitch, changing colour as and when you like. If a yarn you need to pick up is at the opposite end, push all the stitches to the other end of the circular needle. Then work the next row in the same stitch as the last.

Textured stocking-stitch stripe

To add a different texture as well as colour, use a different type of yarn when you add a stripe. This stripe is worked with a chunky yarn and a 4ply yarn. Work in stocking stitch (st st) on circular needles.

People cushion cover

Impress everyone by creating this fun, detailed cushion cover using the Fair Isle, intarsia and moss (seed) stitching techniques

Difficulty ★★★★☆

Skills needed
Knitting in rows
Fair Isle
Intarsia
Moss (seed) stitch
Seaming
Buttonholes
Working from a chart

Finished measurements
Made to fit a 40x40 cm (16x16 ins) cushion insert

Yarn
For this pattern you will need eight different colours, as listed below, in Aran weight. In this example Drops Alaska and Drops Nepal.
Colour 1: Light Grey; 4 x balls.
Colour 2: Off White; 1 x ball.
Colour 3: Light Olive; 1 x ball.
Colour 4: Dark Turquoise; 1 x ball.
Colour 5: Cerise; 1 x ball.
Colour 6: Baby Cashmerino Peach Melba (yarn used double); 1 x ball.
Colour 7: Goldenrod; 1 x ball.
Colour 8: Orange; 2 x balls.

Tension (Gauge)
18.5 sts and 25 rows = 10cm (4in) in st st using 5mm needles
20.5 sts and 23 rows over Fair Isle.

Needles
5mm (US 8) needles.

Other supplies
40cm (15¾in) x 40cm (15¾in) cushion pad
5 x medium sized buttons

People cushion cover
Make in one piece
Using col 4, cast (bind) on 77 sts.
Row 1: K1, *P1, K1 to end.
Row 2: As row 1.
These 2 rows form moss (seed) st. Cont in moss (seed) st as set for a further 5 rows. Change to col 1.
Work in st st stripes as follows;
Row 1: K with col 1.
Row 2: K1, P to last st, K1 with col 1.
Rows 3 and 4: As rows 1 and 2.
Row 5: K with col 8.
Row 6: K1, P to last st, K1.
Repeat these 6 rows 12 times more. Change to col 1.
Next 2 rows; with col 1, K, increasing 6 sts evenly across first row. (83 sts)

Start front
With RS facing, and keeping continuity of K1 at beginning and end of each row, work 2 rows st st.

Note: When following charts, work from right to left on RS rows and left to right on WS rows. Charts 1, 2, 3 and 5 are worked in Fair Isle, chart 4 in intarsia.

Start pattern
Row 1: K2 with col 1, following row 1 of Chart 1 work the 18sts 4 times, then rep the first 7 sts once more, K2 with col 1.
Row 2: K1, P1 with col 1, then following row 2 of Chart 1 work the last 7 sts once, then work the 18sts 4 times, with col 1 P1, K1.
Rows 3-10: Continue to follow Chart 1 as set, until 10 rows have been worked.
Rows 11 and 12: Work 2 rows st g st col 1.
Row 13: K1 with col 1, following row 1 of Chart 2 work these 9 sts 9 times, K1 col 1.
Row 14: K1 with col 1, following row 2 of Chart 2 work these 9 sts 9 times, K1 col 1.
Rows 15-17: Continue to follow Chart 2 for a further 3 rows as set.
Rows 18 and 19: st st col 1.
Rows 20-31: as rows 1-12.

Row 32: K1 with col 1, following row 1 of Chart 3 work these 9 sts 9 times, K1 col 1.

Rows 33-36: continue to follow Chart 3 for a further 4 rows, as set.

Rows 37 and 38: With col 2 work 2 rows in st st.

Row 39: K3 with col 2, following row 1 of chart 4, (using intarsia method) work these 22 sts 3 times, then rep the first 11 sts once more, K3 with col 2.

Row 40: K1, P2 with col 2, then following row 2 of Chart 4 work the last 11 sts once, then work the 22 sts 3 times, then P2, K1 with col 2

Rows 41-56: Continue to follow chart 4 as set, until 18 rows have been worked.

Rows 57 and 58: With col 2 work 2 rows in st st.

Row 59: K1 with col 2, following row 1 of chart 5 work these 9 sts 9 times, K1 with col 2.

Rows 60-63: continue to follow chart 5 as set for a further 4 rows.

Rows 64 and 65: With col 1 work 2 rows in st st.

Rows 66- 77: as rows 1-12.

Rows 78-82: as rows 13-17.

Rows 83 and 84: With col 1 work 2 rows in st st.

Rows 85-94: as rows 1-10.

Continuing to work with col 1 only, work 2 rows in st st.

Next row (dec): Knit, decreasing 6 sts evenly across row. (77 sts).

Next Row (WS): Purl to create fold line. Change to col 4.

Knit 1 row.

Work 3 rows in moss (seed) st.

Buttonhole row: moss (seed) 7 sts *k2tog, yon, moss 13; rep from * to last 10 sts, k2tog, yon, moss (seed) to end.

Work a further 3 rows moss st.

Cast (bind) off.

Making up

Press under a damp cloth, blocking to correct measurements.

Sew side seams.

Sew buttons on to correspond with buttonholes.

Chart 1

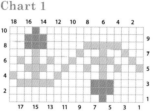

Chart 2

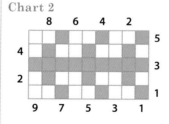

Chart 5

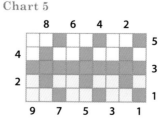

Chart 4

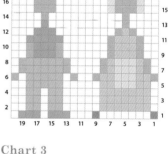

Chart 3

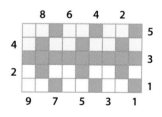

Key:

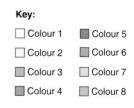

☐ Colour 1   ■ Colour 5
☐ Colour 2   ■ Colour 6
▨ Colour 3   ☐ Colour 7
▨ Colour 4   ▨ Colour 8

Did you know?

Queen Victoria was an avid knitter throughout her life. During her reign the popularity of handcrafts increased significantly.

Short row shaping

Learn how to create definition in garments by adding shape and smoothing edges — all you need to master is the technique of working partial rows

The technique of short row shaping is used in a multitude of patterns to structurally shape knitting. Whether to add more definition to the bust of a sweater, create a rounded shoulder, or add the perfect curve to the heel of a sock, this simple but effective technique will deliver great results. While it is mainly seen on a stocking stitch base, it can also be quite effective when used on a garter stitch.

Also called 'turning', the technique is achieved by working the stitches part way along a row, then turning your work and working back along the stitches just worked. This means that those stitches have been worked for two more rows compared to the rest of the

knitting. Depending on the pattern, you may knit partway and return for many rows, or just work a few short rows at regular intervals. One problem that is caused by working short rows is that a hole will form where the knitting has been turned, depending on the pattern worked. Below are two ways to avoid holes.

"Add more definition to the bust of a sweater or create a rounded shoulder"

Tie or Wrap (and turn, w&t)
Start shaping and wrapping your stitches

01 Short row shaping
Work the number of stitches stated on the pattern for the short row shaping. Take the yarn to the other side of the work through the needles. Slip the next stitch purlwise (pwise), then take the yarn to the original side of work and turn. Sometimes, slipping the first stitch purlwise gives a smoother finish.

02 Wrapped stitches
Once you have completed the short row, when working across all stitches, the wrap may interfere with your pattern. Work to the stitch that has been wrapped and work it together with the stitch that has been wrapped by inserting the needle into the loop of the wrap from underneath and then into the stitch.

Use 'over' to avoid holes
Make sure it joins up

01 Turn position
Work the number of stitches to the turn position. Take the yarn to the other side of the work though the needles, then bring the yarn back to the original side over the needle (creating an 'over'). Continue to work the short row. On the next long row, if working knit stitches, knit the yarn over and the next stitch together.
On a purl row, drop the 'over', slip the next stitch, pick up the over and place it on the left needle, then purl the over and the slipped stitch together.

Bluebird of happiness

**Put the techniques into practice and follow this pattern
to make a soft children's toy — perfect for newborn babies**

Difficulty ★★★☆☆

Skills needed
Increasing
Decreasing
Pick up and knit
Knitting in rounds
Wrap and turn (short rows)

Finished measurements
10cm (4in) long from beak to tail

Yarn
For this pattern you shall require a DK
(worsted) yarn. In the example, Red Heart
Super Saver yarn was used. You will need
a total of 27m (30 yards).

Tension (Gauge)
Gauge is not important with toys.
Changing yarn weight or needle size will
only serve to make your finished object
smaller or larger.

Needles
3.5mm (US 4) 4x double pointed needles
(DPNs)

Other supplies
Tapestry needle
Stuffing

Bluebird of happiness
Note: Work begins at neckline.
Cast (bind) on 18 stitches onto 3 DPNs,
join in the round and work the following
rounds:
Rnd 1: K all sts.
Rnd 2 (inc): (M1, K6), rep to end of rnd
— 21 sts.
Rnd 3: K all sts.
Rnd 4 (inc): (M1, K7) rep to end of rnd
— 24 sts.
Rnd 5: K all sts.
Rnd 6 (inc): (M1, K8) rep to end of rnd
— 27 sts.

Rnd 7: K all sts.
Rnd 8: K3, w&t, P6, w&t, K3.
Rnd 9: K4, w&t, P8, w&t, K4.
Rnd 10: K5, w&t, P10, w&t, K5.
Rnd 11: K6, w&t, P12, w&t, K6.
Rnd 12: K7, w&t, P14, w&t, K7.
Rnd 13: K8, w&t, P16, w&t, K8.
Rnd 14 (dec): K1, k2tog, K to last 3 sts in
rnd, ssk, K1 — 25 sts.
Rnds 15—19: Rep Rnd 14 — 15 sts.
Rnd 20: K all sts.
Rnd 21 (dec): Rep Rnd 14 — 13 sts.
Rnd 22: K all sts.
Rnd 23 (dec): Rep Rnd 14 — 11 sts
Rnd 24: K all sts.
Rnd 25 (dec): Rep Rnd 14 — 9 sts.
Rnd 26: K all sts.
Rnd 27 (dec): Rep Rnd 14 — 7 sts.
Rnd 28: K all sts.
Cut the yarn, thread end into a tapestry
needle, and slip through remaining live
stitches. Do not pull closed yet.

Head
Beginning just to the right of the first cast
(bind) on stitch (centre of the bird's chest),
pick up and knit 18 stitches, 1 in each of
the original cast (bind) on stitches, then
work the rounds below. (Round 3 should
be worked exactly as written; 2 of the
stitches will be wrapped 3 times each.)
Rnd 1: K all sts.

Rnd 2: K all sts.
Rnd 3: K12, w&t, P6, w&t, K6, w&t, P6,
w&t, K6, w&t, P6, w&t, K12.
Rnd 4: K all sts.
Rnd 5: K all sts.
Rnd 6 (dec): (K1, k2tog) to end of rnd —
12 sts.
Rnd 7 (dec): (K2tog) to end of rnd — 6
sts.
Rnd 8 (dec): (K2tog) to end of rnd — 3
sts.

Making up
Cut yarn, thread end into a tapestry
needle, and slip through remaining live
stitches. Pull tightly closed and secure.
   Using the end of a straight needle, stuff
the bluebird's head and body through
open end at tail, being mindful of his
graceful lines. Do not stuff the tail; rather,
flatten it out and bend in an upward
direction.
Pull yarn tightly closed and secure.
Darn any holes; weave in loose ends.

Fixing a dropped stitch

It's easy to panic when you drop a stitch, but there's really no need to worry, as it is very simple to fix

If a stitch drops off one of your needles, don't worry. This is called a dropped stitch and there are steps you can take to get it back on the needle. If you see the stitch come off the needle, fix it immediately by picking it up with the tip of whichever needle it has dropped from, being sure to keep the right leg of the stitch on top. However, if the stitch has begun to unravel from the work, secure it with a crochet hook or cable needle as soon as you can to prevent any further damage. If a dropped stitch is left, it can unravel all the way to the cast (bind)-on edge. When this happens, you are left with a vertical column of horizontal strands that used to be stitches — this is called a ladder, as the unravelled stitches look like rungs on a ladder. Follow these steps to get your stitches back where they're supposed to be.

Pick up a dropped stitch
Make it look as though it never dropped off

01 Locate your dropped stitch
If your dropped stitch has only unravelled by one row and you have what looks like one rung on a ladder, the solution is very simple.

02 Pick up the stitch
With the left-hand needle (you can also use the right to help you if it's easier), pick up the dropped stitch, from front to back, leaving the strand at the back of the work.

03 Get the strand
Now move the strand onto the left-hand needle, also from front to back.

04 Fix the stitch
Move the dropped stitch (the first one you picked up) off the needle, making sure you lift it over the strand. This has remade the stitch that was dropped, and you can continue knitting.

Fix a ladder
Get your stitches back on track

01 Crochet hook
If the stitch has unravelled even further and you have a ladder, it is going to be a bit trickier to fix, but uses the same technique as fixing one rung of a dropped stitch. After you have secured the stitch to stop it unravelling further, you'll need to get a crochet hook to fix the error.

02 Grab the stitch
With the right side (RS) of your work facing you, put the crochet hook through the dropped stitch, from front to back. If you need to, pull the knitting apart slightly so that you can better see the ladder of strands.

03 Begin the climb
Put the crochet hook underneath the first strand and hook it.

04 Make the stitch
Pull the strand through the dropped stitch with the crochet hook, making sure the dropped stitch leaves the hook. You have now corrected one row.

05   Keep hooking the strands through to make new stitches, being sure to work in order. When you have completed the ladder and come to the final stitch, slip it off the crochet hook and onto the left-hand needle. The mistake is corrected.

TOP TIP
Don't forget to work in a pattern. If you're fixing a ladder that has knit and purl stitches, make sure the knit side is facing you as you complete each row.

Finishing

Complete your projects in style

"When choosing which buttonhole to work, consider the stretch of the fabric"

Picking up stitches

To add borders to your finished work, you will first need to pick up the stitches on the edge that you wish to 'finish'

I f the pattern you're following calls for a border, you may find that you need to pick up the edges along your finished piece of work. This is a technique that even experienced knitters can find challenging, so careful preparation and lots of practice will help. When picking up stitches, always have the right side (RS) of the yarn facing you, as it creates a ridge on the wrong side (WS). If you're following a pattern, it should specify which size needle to pick up the stitches with and the required number of stitches for you to pick up. In these instructions a contrasting colour yarn has been used to demonstrate the technique, however, picking up stitches in a matching yarn will hide any imperfections. If your pattern calls for a contrasting border, start with the new colour on the first row of the border.

"This is a technique that even experienced knitters can find challenging"

Along a cast (bind) on/off edge
From front to back

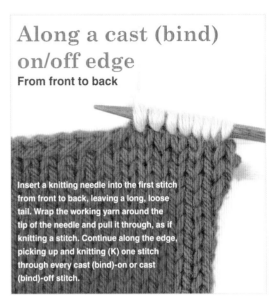

Insert a knitting needle into the first stitch from front to back, leaving a long, loose tail. Wrap the working yarn around the tip of the needle and pull it through, as if knitting a stitch. Continue along the edge, picking up and knitting (K) one stitch through every cast (bind)-on or cast (bind)-off stitch.

Along row ends
Mark and pick up stitches

01 Mark stitches

On light-weight or medium-weight yarn, pick up about 3 stitches for every 4 row ends. Mark out which stitches you are going to pick up by placing a pin on the 1st of every 4 row ends. You will only pick up the stitches in between the pins.

02 Pick up stitches

Insert the needle tip through the centre of the edge stitches and pick them up in the same way as for along a cast (bind)-on edge. Make sure you skip each 4th row end.

With a crochet hook
Hook stitches and transfer them

01 Hook stitches
Being sure to use a crochet hook that fits through the stitches, insert the hook through the first stitch. Wrap the hook behind and around the yarn from left to right and pull through.

02 Transfer to needle
When a new loop has been formed on the crochet hook, transfer it onto a knitting needle. Repeat this for all stitches.

Picking up stitches around a curve
You'll most often need to pick up stitches on a curve around armbands and necklines

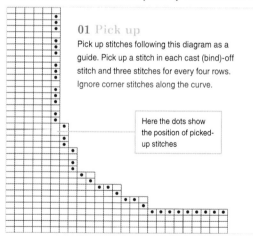

Here the dots show the position of picked-up stitches

01 Pick up
Pick up stitches following this diagram as a guide. Pick up a stitch in each cast (bind)-off stitch and three stitches for every four rows. Ignore corner stitches along the curve.

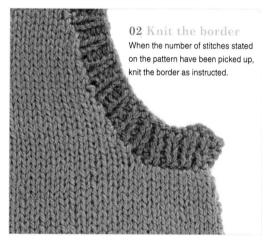

02 Knit the border
When the number of stitches stated on the pattern have been picked up, knit the border as instructed.

Tips for picking up stitches

- Always catch a whole loop; just working into the edge loop can cause holes and distort knitting, and doesn't hide the edge.
- Try using a knitting needle one or two sizes smaller than the needle used to make the project to pick up stitches.
- When picking up stitches ensure the right side is facing you.
- Be careful not to split the yarn when inserting the needle into the fabric.

- The first row you work after picking up stitches will be a wrong side row.
- If working the border in a contrasting colour to the main piece, pick up stitches in the shade that worked the main piece, as this will hide imperfections.

Buttonholes

It's more important than you might first think to find the best buttonhole for your project. Our guide will talk you through the various options and advantages

Buttons are a very common fastening for hand-knitted projects. Whether on the front of a cardigan, the neckline of a sweater or to close a bag, buttons not only offer a secure closure, but with the myriad of styles available, they can also add a decorative element to the finished piece.

The most popular form of buttonhole is the eyelet hole, usually created by working 2 stitches together (k2tog), then forming a yarn over (yo). This creates an elastic hole to pass a button through. However, over the next six pages, we'll show you how to make the various buttonholes available to knitters and what projects they are best suited to.

When choosing which buttonhole to work, take into account the stretch of the fabric; sometimes knitting a strand of colour-matched sewing thread just on the buttonhole stitches can help to reinforce the hole. Also, if you have worked a horizontal buttonhole, the button will rarely sit in the centre of the hole; instead it will move to the outer side. Often, buttonhole bands and button bands (the part that the buttons are sewn onto) will be added to the garment separately.

Loose-fitting jackets made in thicker yarns will need fewer buttons than a fitted cardigan worked in fine yarn such as 4ply. There are no rules for button placement, but they must be evenly and consistently spaced. Sometimes, groups of buttons can make a great feature.

> *"When choosing which buttonhole to work, consider the stretch of the fabric"*

Spacing buttons

To have a well-balanced closing, it is important to evenly space buttonholes

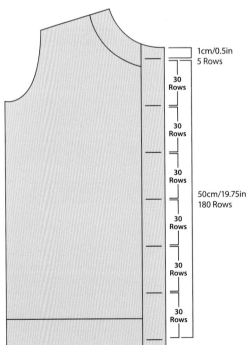

1cm/0.5in
5 Rows

30 Rows

30 Rows

30 Rows

50cm/19.75in
180 Rows

30 Rows

30 Rows

30 Rows

How many buttons?

The majority of patterns you will work, will state exactly how many buttons you will need, and state in the instructions where and how to make the buttonholes. However, you may have a pattern that simply states 'evenly space buttons'. To do this, first work the edge that you will sew the buttons on to, before working the buttonhole band.

On the buttonhole band, place a pin or loose stitch of contrasting yarn 1cm (0.4in) from the top of the band and another 1cm (0.4in) from the bottom — this marks the top and bottom buttons. Now measure the gap between, and evenly space pins to show the other button positions.

Based on the button band, make a note of how many rows and stitches need to be worked between each buttonhole.

Sewn button loops
Use this method to add button loops to a finished piece of knitting

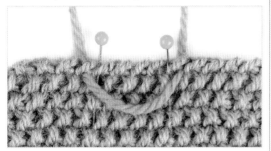

01 Form a loop
Mark the position and width of the loops with pins. Thread a tapestry needle with matching or contrasting yarn, and pass it through the knitting, back to front, pulling it most of the way, but leaving a small tail. Hold the tail in place as you take the needle back through the knitting at the 2nd pin position to form a loop.

02 Create a double loop
Take the needle from back to front through the 1st pin position again to give you a double loop of yarn with a short tail (this tail will be hidden when the loop is worked).

03 Pass the needle through
Pass the needle through the yarn loop, around the back, and through the loop you have just created. Pull tight. Continue to cover the doubled yarn loop and tail. Once finished, pass the needle through a few of the stitches on the loop and cut the yarn.

Knitted button loop
If you can't sew a button loop, knit a loop and attach it with securing stitches

01 Cast (bind) on and off
In the same or contrasting yarn as the knitted piece, cast (bind) on the number of stitches to match the length of loop you wish to create. Now cast (bind) off all stitches.

02 Attach the loops
First, folding the loop in half, attach the ends of the loop to the edge of the reverse side of your knitting.

TOP TIP

Button choice
Match the size of the button to the weight of the yarn. Delicate yarns suit small, pretty patterned buttons, while heavier fabrics, worked in yarns such as Aran or Chunky really complement toggles, leather or wooden buttons.

Simple or chain eyelet
Ideal for making a small buttonhole

Open eyelet buttonhole
A variation on the previous buttonhole

01 Wind the yarn over the needle
Work along the row to the position of the buttonhole. Wind the yarn over the needle (yon).

01 Wind the yarn
Knit to the position of the buttonhole. Wind the yarn over the needle (yon) from front to back, slip 1 stitch (sl1), knitwise (kwise). Knit the next stitch.

02 Work 2 stitches together
Knit the next 2 stitches together (k2tog). You can see that the yarn over (yo) has created a hole in your knitting and an extra stitch on your needle. By working 2 stitches together you have kept the number of stitches on the needle the same.

02 Pass over
Pass the slipped stitch over (psso) the knit stitch. (You've added a stitch with the yarn over (yo), but taken one away with the pass slipped stitch over decrease.)

03 Purl the yarn over
When you work the next row, simply purl the yarn over (yo) as you would normally. This type of buttonhole is perfect for baby clothes, or when a small button is required.

03 Purl the yarn over
When you work the next row, make sure you purl the yarn over (yo) as you would normally.

Reinforced eyelet
This method creates a strong, neat buttonhole

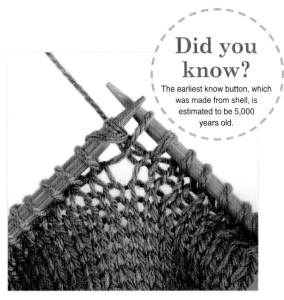

01 Work the row

When working on a stocking stitch (st st) background, knit to the position of the buttonhole and yarn over needle (yon), taking the yarn front to back, then over the needle. Work as stated to the end of the row. On the next row, purl to the yon stitch, slip it purlwise (pwise), then create another yon. Work the rest of the row as stated.

02 Slip the stitch

When you reach the yarn over needles (yons) on the next row, slip the stitch directly before the yons knitwise (kwise). You should knit the 2 yons together, but don't slip them off the needle.

03 Knit 3 stitches together

Pass the slipped stitch over the stitch just made, as you would in a cast (bind) off. Finally knit 3 stitches together (the yarn overs (yos) plus the next stitch on the needle).

04 Stronger eyelet

The eyelet you have created looks just the same as the simple eyelet, but will be stronger. This makes it a great option for children's knits, or garments that will get a lot of wear.

Horizontal one-row buttonhole
Start working this buttonhole on the right side. It is stronger than most holes, with little give

01 Work the yarn through and back
Work to the point in the row for the buttonhole. Bring the yarn through the needles to the front of the work, slip the next stitch purlwise (pwise), and take the yarn back (yb).

02 Slip and pass the stitches
Slip the next stitch purlwise (pwise), then pass over the previously slipped stitch (sl st). Continue to do this until the stated number of stitches have been slipped and passed. Slip the last stitch on the right needle back on to the left needle.

03 Cast (bind) on
Turn your work so that the wrong side is facing, and using the cable cast (bind) on method, cast (bind) on the same number of stitches that were passed over. Cast (bind) on an extra stitch, but before transferring it to the left needle, make sure that you bring the yarn forward (yf), and add a stitch to the left needle.

04 Continue the row
Turn the work and slip the 1st stitch knitwise (kwise). Pass the next stitch over this, and continue to work the rest of the row as stated.

Horizontal buttonhole – buttonhole cast (bind) on

Use a sturdier cast (bind) on to create a sturdy horizontal buttonhole

01 Cast (bind) off

With the right side facing, work to the buttonhole position. Work another 2 stitches, and pass the 1st over the 2nd. Continue to cast off the stated number of stitches. Slip the next stitch knitwise (kwise) onto the right needle and pass over the last cast off loop. Pulling yarn with some tension (gauge), continue the rest of the row as stated.

02 Wind the yarn

On the next row, work to the buttonhole cast (bind) off section. Dropping the left needle, hold the yarn in your right hand, and with your left thumb pointing down, wind the yarn from back to front around thumb. Bringing the thumb to an upright position, you have twisted the loop. Insert the tip of the right needle into the loop.

03 Pull the yarn tight

Wind the yarn around the tip of the right needle from back to front, and then moving the thumb, take the loop over the end of the right needle. Remove your thumb and pull the yarn tightly, holding the stitch in place with your finger if necessary.

04 Continue the row

Continue to make stitches in this way until you have replaced the required number of stitches. Work to the end of the row as stated.

Vertical button hole
You will need a stitch holder to help you create this buttonhole

01 Slip onto a stitch holder
For ease, instructions will assume the pattern is worked in stocking stitch (st st). With right side facing, work to the position of the buttonhole. Slip the rest of the stitches from the left-hand needle onto a stitch holder.

02 Work the stitches
Turn the work, slip the 1st stitch purlwise (pwise), then purl the rest of the row. Work the stitches that fall to the right of the buttonhole for the required number of rows as stated on your pattern, ending on a wrongside row, slipping the 1st stitch of all purl rows. Cut the yarn. Slip the stitches from the holder onto the empty needle, then slip the stitches from the right side of the buttonhole onto the stitch holder.

03 Create a make 1
Slip the 1st stitch knitwise (kwise) and create a make 1 increase (m1) (see page 35). Knit to the end of the row. Continue to work in stocking stitch (st st), slipping the 1st stitch of all knit rows, until you have worked the same number of rows as the previous side ending with a wrong side row. Cut the yarn.

04 Restore the correct number of stitches
Transfer all of the stitches to the same needle and in the correct order, ready with the right side facing. Knit to buttonhole, knitting the two hole-edge stitches together in order to restore the correct number of stitches on the needle.

Sloping (diagonal) buttonhole
This buttonhole adds a decorative finish to a project

TOP TIP If you would like to stick with convention, then place men's buttonholes on the left side and women's on the right.

01 Purl to the end
On a right side row, knit to the buttonhole position. Transfer the stitches left on the left-hand needle to a stitch holder. Turn your knitting and *slip the 1st stitch, purlwise (pwise). Wind the yarn over the needle (yon) from the back to the front and purl to the end of the row.

02 Continue
Turn work and knit to the yarn over (yo) stitch. Knit into the back of the loop, knit the last stitch. Repeating from the * symbol in step 1, continue to work the required number of rows.

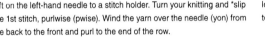

03 Transfer the other stitches
Leaving a long tail, cut your yarn, place the stitches just worked on a stitch holder, and transfer the 1st set of stitches back onto your needle. With the right side facing, join in yarn, slip 1 stitch (sl1) knitwise (kwise) and create a make 1 increase (m1). Knit to the end of the row.

04 Work the two sides together
On the next row, *purl to the last 3 stitches, purl 2 together (p2tog), purl the last stitch. Knit the next row, slipping the 1st stitch. Repeat from * until the same number of rows have been worked. Cut the yarn. Transfer the stitches back to the needles with the right side facing. Rejoin the yarn. Knit across row to the buttonhole, work the two side edges together.

Pockets

Whether practical or decorative, there are several ways you can insert a pocket into your project

Here we will look at three of the most common ways of adding a pocket to a knitted project or garment. First is the patch pocket: this is added to your knitting once you have finished it. You can add lots of fun to sweaters and cushion covers by working the pocket in an outrageously contrasting yarn, or even working an interesting shape such as a hexagon, closing all but the top side. To work this pocket you will pick up the bottom edge of stitches then work the panel, which will be sewn on later.

Second is the horizontal slit pocket — many find this neater than the patch pocket because the lining is worked separately and the opening is more discreet. It is the pocket that most patterns will call for. The example shown here shows the lining worked in a contrast colour to more clearly show you the stitches, but you can also work it in the same colour as the rest of the pattern.

This type of pocket is perfect for a patterned background, such as cable. Make a feature of the pocket and incorporate a cable running up the middle.

Finally, we have a pocket that is perfect for cardigans and hooded projects, the vertical pocket. This is usually inset on the edge of a panel with the pocket lining worked at the same time.

"Add lots of fun by working the pocket in an outrageously contrasting yarn"

Patch pocket

Add these to your garments for a wonderful finishing touch

01 Position the panel

Once you have completed the garment panel, use a contrasting yarn and tapestry needle to 'tack' and outline the pocket position.

02 Secure it

Thread the end of the yarn you are using for the pocket, take it through the right side of the knitted panel, at the bottom-left corner of the pocket position, and secure it on the wrong side. With a crochet hook, insert the point into the centre of the 'v' of the first stitch on the bottom-right corner of the pocket position. Take the point below the top loop, then back out to the front. Catch the yarn with the end of the hook and pull through to make a loop.

03 Work it up

Transfer the loop to a knitting needle, keeping an even tension. Continue to pick up stitches with the crochet hook and transferring them to your needle until you have the required number of stitches on your needle. Turn the work, so that the needle with stitches to be worked is in your left hand, and starting with a wrong side row, work the number of rows required. You can add a garter stitch or ribbed welt to the top of the pocket for a neat finish.

04 Finish it off

Gently block the pocket panel, avoiding the welt, and pin in place on the knitted panel. Remove the tacked stitches. Join the sides to the panel with mattress stitch, darn in ends.

Horizontal slit project
Create this charmingly discreet pocket

01 Work on position

First work the pocket lining as stated in your pattern — this will generally be 2 stitches wider than the cast (bind)-off edge of the pocket. You can leave this panel on a spare needle or stitch holder until you are ready to work it. Now knit to the pocket position and with the right side of the work facing you, cast (bind) off the required number of stitches. Continue to work to the end of the row.

02 Continue the rows

On the next row, work to 1 stitch before the cast (bind) off stitches, and with the wrong side of the pocket lining facing you, work together the last stitch and the first stitch of the pocket lining, then work across all but the last stitch of the pocket. Work this stitch together with the first stitch of the main piece, then work across the rest of main piece stitches.

03 Attach the sides and base

Once you have finished working the garment, attach the sides and base of the pocket to the wrong side of your work.

04 Or try this variation...

Rather than casting (binding) off the stitches on the first step, transfer the pocket top stitches to a stitch holder. Once you have completed the knitted panel, transfer the pocket top stitches to a needle and work a rib or garter stitch welt.

Inset pocket
Learn how to create this final pocket alternative

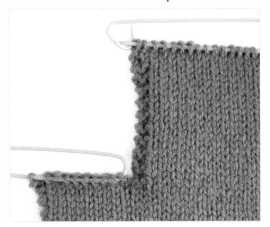

01 Start the pattern

Work your pattern as stated, then on a right-side row, work to the pocket position. Transfer remaining stitches from the left-hand needle to a stitch holder. Turn the work and on the wrong side, knit 2 or 3 stitches to form a garter stitch border, then work to the end of the row. Continue to work the knitted panel until you have worked enough rows for the height of the pocket, keeping the garter stitch edge and ending with a wrong side row. You can keep the stitches worked on a spare needle or transfer them to a stitch holder and cut yarn.

02 Work on the lining

Transfer the stitches from the first stitch holder to a needle ready to work with right side facing. Rejoin yarn and using the cable cast (bind) on method, cast (bind) on the required number of stitches for the pocket lining. Knit across the row, then turn and working on just these stitches, work the same number of rows for the lining as you worked for the front of the pocket. Leave stitches on the needle.

03 Join the lining

To join the pocket lining to the main piece, transfer the stitches from the holder to a needle. With right side facing, work until the same number of stitches that you cast (bound) on for the pocket lining are left on the right needle. With the lining stitches at the back, work together the first 2 stitches of both needles.

04 Finish up

Continue until all stitches have been worked together. Knit to end of row. Once you have completed your knitted panel, you can pin in place the pocket lining and sew it to the front.

Add a picked up/folded hem

**Use this method to create a good thick hem in stocking (stockinette) stitch.
It's ideal for smock type sweaters and loose-fitting sleeve cuffs**

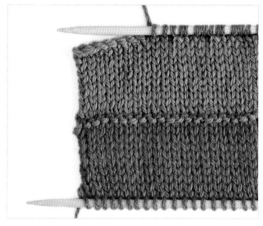

01 Work the hem

Cast (bind) on the number stitches required in the pattern, using a needle one size smaller than you'll use for the main body of the garment. Work the inner hem to the length required, ending on a knit row. If using two colours, change yarn now. Knit the next row (to create a fold line), then change to larger needles and work the same number of rows as worked on the first part of the hem, ending on a purl row.

02 Transfer stitches

With the cast (bind) on edge uppermost, right side (RS) facing and a smaller needle, pick up and knit through the centre of each cast (bind) on stitch using a length of the main body colour yarn. Transfer these stitches so that the point of the needle is facing the opposite direction.

03 Fold the hem

With wrong sides (WS) together, fold the hem and hold both needles in your left hand ready to proceed.

04 Knit stitches together

Rejoin main yarn then insert right needle into the first stitch of both needles. Knit these stitches together. Continue across the row until all stitches have been worked.

05 Finish it

Block hem as per the ballband's instructions.

Picot edge

Use this as an alternative hem for socks, cardigans and more, and you'll get garments with attractive edges

TOP TIP
This type of edge works best in a smooth yarn; it would be lost if worked with fluffy, mohair type haloed yarns.

Creating a picot hem is one of knitting's little tricks. Start off by knitting a few rows, be it in rib or stocking (stockinette) stitch, then on 1 row you alternate working 2 stitches together with a yarn over. Carry on working the following rows in your original stitch, then when you fold the hem at the point of the yarn over row with wrong sides together, you'll see you've created an edge of bumps.

Due to the fact that the edge is folded, it lends itself to be used on a stocking (stockinette) stitch border preventing the knitting from rolling. Also if you use this hem on the base of a garment, the fold lends some weight to the piece, helping it to drape nicely. Unless you have used a ribbed picot hem (such as on the sock pattern on page 52), the hem will not be elastic. So only incorporate this style into loose fitting garments.

01 Start your stitches

After having first cast (bind) on an even number of stitches, work between 5 and 7 rows of stocking (stockinette) stitch. The next row will be a right side row. Work the row as follows: *k2tog, yon. Repeat from * to the end of the row.

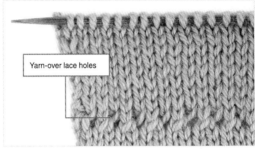

Yarn-over lace holes

02 Purl it

On the next row purl the stitches and the yarn over needles (yon) as you would do normally. Continue to work your pattern as stated.

Tighter hem
Cast (bind) on with a needle size smaller than the pattern suggests to work up to and including the yarn over row.
Then change to the recommended needle size.

03 Making up

When you are at the making up stage, fold the picot hem over at the yarn over needle (yon) row, with the wrong sides (WS) together. Pin the hem in place, ensuring that the cast (bind) on edge lines up with a row of knitting. With a tapestry needle thread with yarn, sew the cast (bind) on edge to the row of knitting by inserting the needle into a loop of the stitch, and then into the corresponding stitch on the cast (bind) on edge. Pull yarn through and continue in this way to the end of the hem.

04 Block it

Gently block, being careful to avoid the folded edge.

Blocking

Set your knitting in place and keep it looking its very best by blocking it with steam or water

O nce you have spent many hours creating your knitting garment or accessories, you'll want it to look good forever. The way to do this is blocking. Essentially you wet the knitted fabric (before or after) pinning it out to the shape and dimensions given in the measurements and let it dry fully. Sometimes you apply heat but it depends on the fibre you have worked with, so check the yarn label.

There are two processes to blocking: dampening the knitted fabric, and pinning it out to the desired dimensions and shape. If you are making up a garment from separate pieces, block each to the stated size on the measurements table of the pattern by measuring and pinning to size each piece. Once all the pieces are dry you will be able neatly join them all to make up the garment.

Tips for blocking

You don't need specialist equipment to block your knitting.

- Pins: You can purchase specific T-pins for blocking your work, but if you're just starting out, regular non-rusting glasshead pins will work just fine.
- Spray bottle: The type you use to spray water on plants or to damp hair before cutting.
- Steam iron: Not used for all fibres. Please read 'How to treat different fibres' section for more details.
- Tape measure: A metal one is best, as over time fabric tape measures have a tendency to stretch.
- Blocking mats: Interlocking foam playmats are ideal, although knitters have been know to block sweater panels over towels pinned to a spare bed.

How to treat different fibres
Check your yarn's ball band for the fibre content

Wool: This is very forgiving. There are three ways to block this: Wet blocking (do not wring the water, as you will damage the fibres) is ideal for heavy patterns such as cable, Steam Blocking, and Pin and Spritz, which is effective on finer tension (gauge) yarns.

Silk: Once wet, silk becomes very fragile. It is best to Pin and Spritz silk knit fabrics.

Nylon, polyester and other man-made fibres: Avoid the steam iron completely as the heat

will damage the fibre structure. It is best to Pin and Spritz.

Cotton: Adding structure during the knitting process is best for cotton. The fibres are inelastic, tend not to hold their shape and have no memory. Steam Blocking is best.

Alpaca and Cashmere: Both of these animal fibres are very delicate indeed. Play it safe with them and Pin and Spritz.

Fibre blends: When there is more than one

fibre making up your yarn, again play it safe and Pin and Spritz.

TOP TIP

Place a piece of chequered cloth between the blocking mat and knitting. Use the straight lines to help you pin out straight edges.

Types of blocking

Here are the three ways to block your knitting. See the opposite page to work out which method would work best for your project

Wet blocking

Immerse your knitted piece into lukewarm or cold water. Gently squeeze out the water, do not wring it as this can damage the connecting fibres. Lay the piece flat on a towel and roll it up like a Swiss roll to squeeze out as much moisture as you can. You may need to repeat this. You can either position your piece on another towel that has been placed on the blocking mat or lay it directly on the mat. Pin it in place and leave it to completely dry.

Steam blocking

Pin your knitted piece out to the dimensions given on the pattern, with your knitted fabric placed right side up. Wet a clean pillowcase or tea towel and wring out any extra moisture. Place this flat on top of your knitting. With your iron on the steam setting, hover it 2cm/0.5in above the knitting; the steam will penetrate the fabric and go through to your knitting. Avoid pressing your iron down, especially on ribbed sections. Once the pillowcase/towel is dry, remove it and leave the knitted piece to cool down and dry out completely overnight.

Pin and Spritz

With the right sides of your pieces facing upwards, pin them into shape and to the dimensions stated on the pattern. With your plant sprayer set to a fine mist, spray your knitting with cold water. You'll find that some fibres will need to be sprayed less than others; wool for example will only need a light mist, while synthetic fibres will require more. Allow the knitting to completely dry away from direct heat and light sources, but preferably in a warm room. This method is perfect for textured knitting, hems and welts.

Pinning out

Take time with this stage for great results

Whether you have wet the fabric first, or will apply moisture after, follow these easy rules. With your pattern to hand place your knitting flat on the blocking mat. Pin all the main points such as top of the shoulders, underarms, neck edges, left and right sides above ribs and cuffs. These should all fit to the measurements given on the pattern. With more pins, secure the fabric between these points at regular intervals. If you are pulling out points, you could be pulling too hard, or don't have enough pins in between. Remember not to put any tension on ribbed sections, as this will cause it to permanently stretch.

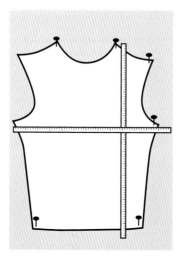

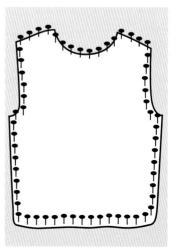

Seaming & edging

Once you've finished knitting the main pieces of your project, you're going to need to join them together

Figure of eight
Neatly secure your yarn before sewing a seam

01 Get started
With the pieces to be joined, side by side, insert the needle from back to front of the corner of the right piece. Next insert the needle from front to back, on the corner of the left-hand piece and pull through.

02 Secure it
Insert the needle from front to back of the right-hand piece again. Pull through to secure.

03 Be ready to work
For mattress stitch and other joins to be completed with the right side facing, insert the needle into the back of the left piece again so that the yarn is at the front ready to work.

Mattress stitch
Create an invisible seam

01 Use the figure of eight
In order to work this stitch, both pieces must have the same number of rows. To start, place pieces next to each other with right side facing. Attach the yarn you are sewing with using a figure of eight.

02 Join the edges
Insert your needle on the first row between the first and second stitch, pick up the strand and pull the yarn through. Repeat this with the second side. Continue in this way until you have joined the edges. You should have an almost invisible seam.

Edge-to-edge seam
Secure the edges side by side

With the wrong side (WS) facing you, place both pieces to be seamed flat on a surface in front of you. Secure the yarn using the figure of eight at the base, then sew along the edges picking up the little bumps on each edge.

Backstitch
Make a secure seam with a backstitch

This is one of the most popular stitches to use for seam knitting. With right sides facing, pin both pieces together to ensure they don't move. Secure yarn with a figure of eight. Working close to the edge of the knitting, make one stitch by inserting the needle front to back. Bring the needle back through to the front and to the left of the first stitch. Take the needle back to the edge of the previous stitch. Continue in this way until the edge is joined.

Whipped stitch seam
Take the yarn over the top to secure it

With right sides (RS) facing, pin both pieces together to ensure they don't move. Secure the yarn with a figure of eight. Working back to front, insert the needle through the centre of the first stitch of each piece. Take the yarn over and continue to stitch in the same way until the piece is joined.

Hints and tips

- Before you join your knitted pieces, block them to the correct dimensions first. Better stitch definition will ensure a neater finish.

- It is always a good idea to pin the edges of the pieces together at regular intervals so that they don't slip. Use long glass-headed pins for the best results.

- If the yarn you have worked with is too slippery or fluffy, use another yarn of the same colour to join the edges.

- Use a blunt, large-eyed tapestry needle to join knitting. A sharp point will split the yarn, making it difficult to pull yarn through.

"Backstitch is one of the most popular stitches to use for seam knitting"

Grafting
Join your fabric invisibly

TOP TIP

Long, glass-headed pins are ideal for holding your pieces of knitting together while joining the seams.

01 Secure the yarn

This creates an almost invisible seam, which works particularly well on shoulder seams. With right sides (RS) facing and both cast (bind)-off edges together, secure the yarn with a figure of eight, then on the bottom piece insert the needle under both strands of the 'v' point from left to right. Repeat on the corresponding stitch on the top piece.

02 Create the invisible join

Ensure that you evenly pull the stitches through so that they blend in with the knitted tension (gauge). Once you have finished you should have and almost invisible join.

Grafting open edges together
Create a seamless finish

01 Start grafting

When joining open edges you must have the same number of stitches on both pieces. First remove the waste yarn or stitch holders and place both pieces on a flat surface with the right sides (RS) facing upwards. Thread your needle with the yarn in the same colour as the piece to be grafted (note: for illustrative purposes, we're showing the joining yarn in a contrast colour).

02 Continue the combination

Insert the needle from behind into the middle of the first 'v' stitch on the left piece. Next, insert the needle from bottom to top behind the two legs of the first 'v' stitch on the right piece. Your yarn should be at the front of the work.

Adding an edging

Work a border separately and then sew it on once you've blocked the knitted pieces

01 Place pins
With right sides together, place the knitted edging on top of the main knitted piece. Place pins at regular intervals to prevent either piece moving.

02 Join together
Starting with a figure of eight at the start of the edging, with even overcast stitches, join the two pieces together.

03 Finish up
Once you have sewn all the edging on, unfold it. For a neat finish, you will need to steam block the join using a damp towel and a steam iron (but only if the yarn allows).

03 Close the gap
Take the needle back to the left piece and insert it from bottom to top beneath the two legs of the next 'v', pulling the yarn through to the right side. As you pull the yarn through, gently close the gap between the two pieces, ensuring that the joining stitch is the same size as the stitches in the main knitted pieces. Take the yarn back to the right piece and continue until you have worked all stitches.

04 Secure it
Secure and darn in the end of the yarn on the wrong side (WS) of the work. With the wrong side of the knitting facing you, unravel and discard the contrast waste yarn. Block the piece as recommended.

Fastenings

Once you've finished your knitted piece, it may need to have some closures added. Whether buttons, poppers or a zip, here's how to add them professionally

Once a garment has been knitted and seamed, adding the fastenings can often come as an afterthought. However, choosing the way to close a garment or accessory should be as integral as choosing the yarn and pattern.

Buttons are the most popular way to fasten garments from cardigans and jackets, to open shoulder seams and cushion covers. Choose your buttons before knitting, so that buttonholes can be made the right size, although it is possible to decided on your buttons afterwards so that you can be sure of an good match with the pattern and yarn.

Poppers are a great way to add a fastening if you want an invisible closure and don't have the option in the pattern to add buttonholes. The size of popper needed will be determined by the weight of the yarn worked and the width of the area to be fastened.

Zips can look great on jackets and for easy closures on cushion covers, however their stiffness does not work too well with the elasticity of hand-knitted fabrics. If you are keen to add a zip, choose a yarn that will not shrink or stretch after wearing or washing. Also be aware that zips come in set lengths — purchase your zip before you start knitting and you can work your pattern to the exact zip length. Zips don't tend to come in a variety of shades, so if you don't have an exact match to your yarn colour, adding a zip in a contrasting shade can make a real feature of it

Sewing buttons
Pick the yarn used for the projects to secure the buttons

01 Secure the yarn
With the yarn/sewing thread doubled, tie a knot at the end. Insert the needle into the right side of the fabric, bring it up from the wrong side and insert into the loop at the end of the yarn by the knot. Pull gently to secure the yarn. On the surface of the fabric, place a cable needle and insert the sewing needle into the hole from the back of the button.

02 Sew the button in place
Sew the button into place in the usual way, keeping the cable needle between the button and the fabric. This ensures that the button isn't sewn on too tightly. Once you have made enough stitches to hold the button do not cut the yarn, but feed the needle through the hole — just don't take it through to the wrong side of the fabric.

03 Strengthen the fastening
With the thread between the fabric surface and the button, lift the button and wind the thread around the connecting stitches several times. This will strengthen the fastening and prevent the button rubbing on the knitted fabric, which could damage it.

Poppers

Place the female side on the outside and the male on the inside

01 The female side

Decide where the poppers is to be placed on the right side (RS) of the inner part of the opening. Evenly space the positions and mark with pins. Taking a needle threaded double with matching thread, secure as for step 1 on attaching buttons. With three or four little stitches, attach the female side popper through the little holes. There is no need to cut the thread between holes, just carry it to the next one.

02 The male side

For the male counterpart of the popper, position them so that they are directly opposite the female side. This time however, when working the little stitches, ensure that the needle and thread do not come through to the right side (RS) of the fabric; instead catch the yarn as you stitch.

Adding a zip

An invisible zip will give the best finish to your knitted garment

02 Pin it

With the zip closed, lay the knitted piece right side (RS) up on a flat surface in position on top of the zip. The knitted edge should cover the teeth of the zip. Pin horizontally at the top, middle and bottom of the zip. Now add pins in the centre of the gaps, then add more pins at the centre of those gaps to ensure even placement. Continue until you have placed enough pins two or three rows apart.

01 Choose the right zip

Finding a zip that is the same length as your knitted piece can be hard. Do not be tempted to stretch or bunch your knitted edge to fit the zip length. Instead, choose your zip first and knit to the same length.

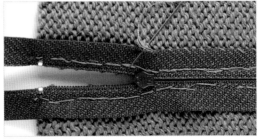

03 Stitch the fabric

With a contrasting yarn or thread, tack the zip to the knitted fabric in a vertical line from top to bottom. Remove pins. Thread a sharp-tipped needle with yarn or matching thread, secure at the bottom hem on the wrong side (WS) and neatly back stitch the fabric to the zip, vertically between the same line of stitches.

04 Finish it up

Turn the knitted fabric over and using the same yarn or thread, attach the edge of the zip fabric to the wrong side (WS) of the knitting, being careful not to take the needle all the way through the knitted fabric, but following the same vertical line of knitted stitches.

Patterns

Apply your new skills in these patterns

Pretty bunting

Whether for a baby's nursery or an outdoor garden party, this pretty bunting will add a vintage feel. Let your imagination run riot and use many different colours

Difficulty ★★★☆☆

Skills needed

Decreasing
Colourwork (intarsia)
Knitting in rows
Working from a chart

Finished measurements

Each pennant measures approx 18x14cm (7x5.5in)

Yarn

For this pattern you will need a DK yarn in two colours. In this example, Patons Diploma Gold DK has been used in Cream and Cyclamen.

Colour 1: Cream 1 x ball
Colour 2: Cyclamen; 1 x ball

Tension (Gauge)

22 stitches and 30 rows = 10cm (4in) in stocking stitch (st st)

Needles

4mm (US 6) needles

Other supplies

Stitch holder
Tapestry needle
Ribbon (optional)

Lou Butt
Lou has been designing knitwear for print and independently for over ten years. She started knitting aged seven when her mum owned a yarn shop in Cornwall, and hasn't put her needles down since. Find her work in Knitted Sock Sensations, Complete Knitting and Socks Rock.

Pretty bunting
Basic pennant

Cast (bind) on 36 sts

Knit 4 rows.

Start decreases

Row 5 (RS): K3, ssk, K to last 5 sts, k2tog, K3. (2 sts decreased)

Row 6 (WS): K3, P to last 3 sts, K3.

Rep rows 5 and 6 until 8 sts rem.

Next row (RS): K2, ssk, k2tog, K2. (6 sts.)

Next row: Knit.

Next row: K1, ssk, k2tog, K1. (4 sts.)

Next row: Knit.

Next row: ssk, k2tog. (2 sts.)

Next row: k2tog.

Cut yarn and pull through stitch to secure.

Making up

Darn in ends and light block on wrong side by pinning to a triangle shape and placing a damp tea towel on the pennant, then lightly brushing over a steam iron. Leave to cool and dry completely before removing.

Tape

Cast (bind) on 3 sts.

Knit every row until tape measures 168cm/66in. This is enough to allow you to space out the pennants with approximately 8cm (3in) between them.

Place sts on a stitch holder, then pin pennants onto knitted tape, leaving 8cm (3in) gaps between each one. You may find that you need to knit more rows, or undo some rows.

Cast (bind) off and darn in ends.

Note: The bunting would also look great attached to pretty ribbon.

Pennant alternatives

Pennant with coloured border

Work as for ***basic pennant*** casting (binding) on in col 1, but on first decrease row add in second yarn colour, work as normal to last 3 sts, join in first yarn colour. So that you don't have to purchase a second ball, locate the yarn end from the centre of the ball to work the second border of colour.

Remember to twist yarns at each colour change to avoid holes.

Continue to work with a col 1 garter stitch border, until 8 sts rem, cut second yarn colour and second col 1 strand. Finish with just one strand of col 1.

Striped pennant

Work as for **basic pennant** casting (binding) on in col 2, but on first decrease row add in second yarn colour after working the first 3 sts, work as normal to last 3 sts, join in first yarn colour. So that you don't have to purchase a second ball, locate the yarn end from the centre of the ball to work the second border of colour.

Remember to twist yarns at each colour change to avoid holes.

Alternate yarn colours every 2 rows, carrying the col 1 and col 2 yarns at the back of the work. (See intarsia technique).

Continue to work with a col 2 garter stitch border, until 8 sts rem, cut col 1 yarn and second col 2 strand. Finish pennant with just one strand of col 2.

Heart pennant

Cast (bind) on in col 1 as for **basic pennant** for 2 sets of decrease rows, until you have 32 sts, ending with a WS row.

In the next row, you add in the second colour and work the chart pattern.

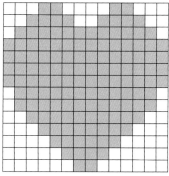

Next row (RS): K3, ssk, K4, work first row of Heart Chart across next 14 sts, K4, k2tog, K3. (2 sts decreased.)

This sets the Heart pattern. Follow chart as set and continue with **basic pennant** pattern. As you work decreases, the col 1 section of the chart will be decreased away: continue to work the col 2 section as set. Once the chart is complete, continue only in col 1 and complete as per the **basic pennant**.

Moon pennant

Cast (bind) on in col 1 as for basic pennant for 2 sets of decrease rows, until you have 32 sts, ending with a WS row.

In the next row, you add in the second colour and work the chart pattern.

Next row (RS): K3, ssk, K4, work first row of Chart across next 10 sts, K4, k2tog, K3. (2 sts dec)

This sets moon pattern. Follow chart

as set and continue with **basic pennant** pattern. As you work decreases, the col 1 section of the chart will be decreased away: continue to work the col 2 section as set. Once the chart is complete, continue only in col 1 and complete as per the **basic pennant**.

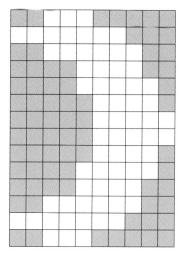

Garter stitch placemat & coaster

Use several different yarns in various different colours and textures to create this simple yet impressive placemat and coaster set

Difficulty ★☆☆☆☆

Skills needed
Knitting in rows

Finished measurements
Placemat: 32cm (12.5in) deep by 38cm (5in) wide
Coaster: 10cm (4in) by 10cm (4in)

Yarn
For this project you shall require an aran weighted yarn. In the example Texere Wild Silk 8, Crystal Palace Cotton Chenille, Rowan Revive DK (doubled), Yeoman Yarns Cotton Club No. 6 Aran and Yeoman Yarns DK Panama (doubled) were used.

Tension (Gauge)
19 stitches and 30 rows = 10cm (4in) in garter stitch

Needles
4.5mm (US 7) needles

Pattern notes
Any aran weight yarns can be used for this project. Finer yarns can be doubled up. The sample uses several different yarns in various colours and textures.

Sian Brown
After doing a Fashion/Textiles BA, Sian worked for companies in London supplying to high street retailers on machine knits. Sian has one book to her name, *The Knitted Home*. Visit her at **sianbrown. com**.

Placemat and coaster

Placemat
With colour 1, cast (bind) on 60 stitches. Work in garter stitch until work measures 38cm (15in) from cast (bind) on edge, bringing in colours 2—7 randomly for whole or part rows.

Cast (bind) off.
Neaten off ends, especially at edges of placemat. Press under a cloth, evening out edges while pressing.

Coaster
With colour 1, cast (bind) on 20 stitches. Work in garter stitch as for placemat until work measures 10cm (4in) from cast (bind) on edge.
Finish as for **placemat**.

Diamond cushion cover

Make this cosy looking cushion cover complete with button holes, seaming and a cable pattern

Difficulty ★★★☆☆

Skills needed
Cables
Knitting in rows
Seaming

Finished measurements
41x41 cm (16x16 in) cushion pad.

Yarn
For this project you will need an Aran weight yarn. In this example Wendy Aran in cream. You will need one 400g ball.

Tension (Gauge)
20sts and 24 rows = 10cm (4ins) over patt.

Needles
2—4mm (US 7)

Other supplies
2 buttons
Darning needle

Thomas B Ramsden
This pattern was kindly supplied by Thomas B Ramsden, a family business who are the suppliers of Wendys and Peter Pan, two of the biggest brands of yarn in the UK. You can find them at **www.tbramsden.co.uk**.

Diamond cushion cover

Front

Cast (bind) on 75 sts, work 2 rows in garter stitch.

Row 1: K1, P1, *m1, K2tbl, p2tog, P1 [K1tbl, P2] twice, K1tbl, P1, p2tog, K2tbl, m1, P1 rep from *to last st, K1

Row 2: K1, *K2, P2, [K2, P1] 3 times, K2, P2, K1 rep from *to last 2 sts, K2

Row 3: K1, P1, *P1, m1, K2tbl, P2, sl, K1, psso, P1, K1tbl, P1, k2tog, P2, K2tbl, m1, P2, rep from * to last st, K1

Row 4: K1, *K3, P2, K2, [P1, K1] twice, P1, K2, P2, K2, rep from *to last 2 sts, K2

Row 5: K1, (K1, yf, K1, yf, K1) in next st, *P2, m1, K2tbl, P2, sl, K1, psso, K1tbl, k2tog, P2, K2tbl, m1, P2, (K1, yf, K1, yf, K1) in next st, rep from *to last st, K1

Row 6: K1, *P5, K3, P2, K2, P3, K2, P2, K3, rep from *to last 6 sts, P5, K1

Row 7: K6, *P3, m1, K2tbl, P2, sl, k2tog, psso, P2, K2tbl, m1, P3, K5, rep from *to last st, K1

Row 8: K1 *P5, K4, P2, K2, P1, K2, P2, K4, rep from *to last 6 sts, P5, K1

Row 9: K1, sl, K1, psso, K1, k2tog, *P2, (K1, yf, K1, yf, K1) in next st, P1, m1, K2tbl, p2tog, K1tbl, p2tog, K2tbl, m1, P1, (K1, yf, K1, yf, K1) in next st, P2 sl, K1, psso, K1, k2tog, rep from *to last st, K1

Row 10: K1, *p3tog, K2, P5, K2, P2, K1, P1, K1, P2, K2, P5, K2, rep from *to last 4 sts, P3tog, K1

Row 11: K1, K1tbl, *P2, K5, P2, m1, K2tbl, p3tog, K2tbl, m1, P2, K5, P2, K1tbl, rep from *to last st, K1

Row 12: K1, *P1, K2, P5, K3, P2, K1, P2, K3, P5, K2, rep from *to last 2 sts, P1, K1

Row 13: K1, K1tbl, *P2, sl, K1, psso, K1, k2tog, P3, K2tbl, P1, K2tbl, P3, sl, K1, psso, K1, k2tog, P2, K1tbl, rep from *to last st, K1

Row 14: K1, *P1, K2, p3tog, K3, P2, K1, P2, K3, P3tog, K2, rep from *to last 2 sts, P1, K1

Row 15: K1, K1tbl, *P2, K1tbl, P1, p2tog, K2tbl, m1, P1, m1, K2tbl, p2tog, P1, K1tbl, P2, K1tbl, rep from *to last st, K1

Row 16: K1, *[P1, K2] twice, P2, K3, P2, K2, P1, K2, rep from *to last 2 sts, P1 K1

Row 17: K1, K1tbl, *P1, k2tog, P2, K2tbl, m1, P3, M1, K2tbl, P2, sl, K1, psso, P1, K1tbl, rep from *to last st, K1

Row 18: K1, *P1, K1, P1, K2, P2, K5, P2, K2, P1, K1, rep from *to last 2 sts, P1, K1

Row 19: K1, K1tbl, *k2tog, P2, K2tbl, m1, P2, (K1, yf, K1, yf, K1) in next st, P2, M1, K2tbl, P2, sl, K1, psso, K1tbl, rep from *to last st, K1

Row 20: K1, *P2, K2, P2, K3, P5, K3, P2, K2, P1, rep from *to last 2 sts, P1, K1

Row 21: K1, k2tog, *P2, K2tbl, m1, P3, K5, P3, m1, K2tbl, P2, sl, k2tog, psso, rep from *to last 22 sts, P2, K2tbl, m1, P3, K5, P3, m1, K2tbl, P2, sl, K1, psso, K1

Row 22: K1, *P1, K2, P2, K4, P5, K4, P2, K2, rep from *to last 2 sts, P1, K1

Row 23: K1, K1tbl, *p2tog, K2tbl, m1, P1, (K1, yf, K1, yf, K1) in next st, P2, sl, K1, psso, K1, k2tog, P2, (K1, yf, K1, yf, K1) in next st, P1, m1, K2tbl, p2tog, K1tbl, rep from *to last st, K1

Row 24: K1, *P1, K1, P2, K2, P5, K2, P3tog, K2, P5, K2, P2, K1, rep from *to last 2 sts, P1, K1

Row 25: K1, p2tog, *K2tbl, m1, P2, K5, P2, K1tbl, P2, K5, P2, m1, K2tbl, p3tog, rep from *to last 26 sts, K2tbl, m1, P2, K5, P2, K1tbl, P2, K5, P2, m1, K2tbl, p2tog, K1,

Row 26: K1 *K1, P2, K3, P5, K2, P1, K2, P5, K3, P2, rep from *to last 2 sts, K2

Row 27: K1, P1, *K2tbl, P3, sl, K1, psso, K1, k2tog, P2, K1tbl, P2, sl, K1, psso, K1, k2tog, P3, K2tbl, P1, rep from *to last st, K1

Row 28: K1, *K1, P2, K3, p3tog, K2, P1, K2, p3tog, K3, P2, rep from *to last 2 sts, K2

From Row 1 to 28th row (inclusive) forms patt. Keeping continuity of patt (throughout) cont until work measures approximately 41 cm (16 ins), ending with 14th row of patt.

Cast (bind) off in patt.

Back (in 2 pieces)

Cast (bind) on 75 sts Work 2 rows in garter stitch.

Work rows 1 - 28 twice.

Change to K1, P1 rib and work 4 rows.

Next Row (Buttonhole row): Rib 25, yo, rib 2tog, rib 21, yo, rib 2tog, rib 25.

Work 3 more rows in rib.

Cast (bind) off.

2nd Piece

Sing 4mm Needles cast (bind) on 75 sts Work 8 rows in K1, P1 rib

Cont in patt, starting with row 5 to 28. Rep rows 1-28 until the two pieces of the Back when overlap rib section are put together match the Front, ending with a 14th patt row

Cast (bind) off in patt.

Making up

Overlap the rib sections of Back cushion cover together and tack in place. Sew Front and Back together by top sewing. Remove tacking sts. Sew on buttons. Block.

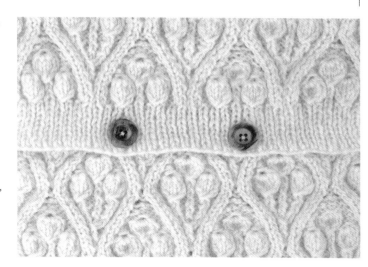

Hearts Fair Isle tea cosy & hot water bottle cover

Now it's time to really put your skills to the test and practise some of the harder techniques you've learned by creating a fetching tea cosy and hot water bottle cover

"For this pattern you will need 7 different colours"

Difficulty ★★★★★

Skills needed
Knitting in rows
Fair Isle
Seaming

Finished measurements
Tea Cosy: 23cm (9ins) wide x 20.5cm (8ins) deep.
Hot Water Bottle Cover:
20.5cm (8ins) wide x 30.5cm (12ins) deep.

Yarn
For this pattern you will need 7 different colours, as listed below, in Aran weight. In this example Drops Alaska and Drops Nepal. Amounts are the same for both projects unless otherwise stated.
Colour 1: Nepal; Light Grey Green; 1 x ball. (You will need 2 x balls for the Hot Water Bottle.)
Colour 2: Alaska; Mid Purple; 1 x ball.
Colour 3: Nepal; Light Olive; 1 x ball.
Colour 4: Alaska; Red; 1 x ball.
Colour 5: Alaska; Turquoise; 1 x ball.
Colour 6: Alaska; Deep Purple; 1 x ball.
Colour 7: Nepal; Goldenrod; 1 x ball.

Tension (Gauge)
Work 18 sts and 24 rows in st st to measure 10x10cm (4x4in) using 5mm (US 8) needles, or size required to obtain correct tension.

Needles
5mm (US 8).

TOP TIP

If there is an even amount of stitches per row, you will start with alternate knit and purl stitches each row.

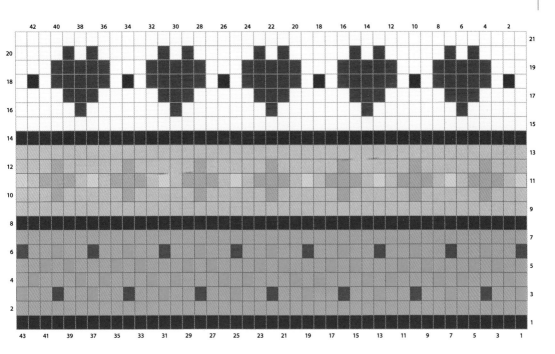

Hearts Fair Isle tea cosy
Front
With col 6, cast (bind) on 45 sts.

Knit 4 rows.

Row 1 (WS): K1 col 3, P43 sts of chart 1 for front, K1.

Rows 2-20; Cont to follow 43 sts chart as set, until 21 rows of the chart have been completed, keeping K1 at each end of every row.

Rows 21-34; Starting with a P row, work rows 1 to 14 once more.

*Row 35; Join col 1, and P 1 row. Cont with col 1, as follows:

Knit 2 rows.

Eyelet row (RS): K3, *K2tog, yo, K4* rep between * 7 times.

Knit 7 rows.

Break off col 1.

Change to col 6. K 1 row.

Cast (bind) off kwise.*

Back
With col 6, cast (bind) on 45 sts.
Knit 4 rows.

Row 1 (WS): K1, P across 43 sts chart 2,

K 1 col 6.

Rows 2-34; Cont to follow chart for back until 34 rows have been worked, keeping K1 at each end of every row.

Complete as for front * to *.

Making up
Press pieces under a damp cloth.

Sew side seams, leaving gaps for handle and spout.

Tie
Cut 6 lengths of yarn in cols 1, 2 and 3, 75cm (30in) long. Plait to form a tie, and thread through eyelets.

Key:

- ☐ Colour 1
- ☐ Colour 2
- ☐ Colour 3
- ■ Colour 4
- ☐ Colour 5
- ■ Colour 6
- ☐ Colour 7

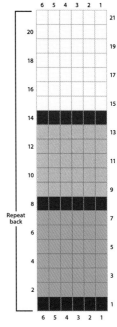

Note
As you work through the charts, join colours as you need them. Knit the first and last stitch of each row in the background colour that you used for that row.

Hearts Fair Isle hot water bottle cover
Front

With col 3, cast (bind) on 45 sts.

Knit 2 rows.

Row 1 (WS): K1, P across 43 sts chart 1, K1.

Rows 2-20: Starting with row 3, K1, work 43 sts across chart 1, K1.

Cont to follow chart until 21 rows of the chart have been worked

Rows 21-41: Starting with a P row, and col 6, work rows 1-21 of chart again, keeping K1 at start and end of each row.

Rows 42-63: Starting with a K row, and col 6, work rows 1-21 of chart again, keeping K1 at start and end of each row.

Row 63 (WS): P 1 row col 6. Break off col 6.

Continue with col 1 only as follows:

Eyelet row (RS): K3, *K2tog, yo, K4* rep

between * 7 times.

Knit 9 rows.

Change to col 6.

Knit 1 row.

Cast (bind) off kwise.

Back

With col 3, cast (bind) on 45 sts.

Knit 2 rows.

Row 2 (WS): K1, P across 43 sts chart 2, repeating the chart across all sts, K 1 col 3.

Rows 3-63: Continue to follow chart 2 for stripe sequence, working K1 st at each end of every row, until 62 rows of the chart have been worked.

Complete as for front from * to *.

Making up

Press both sides under a damp cloth.

Sew side and bottom seams.

Tie

Cut 6 strands of yarn, 2 each in cols 1, 2 and 3, 75cm (30in) long. Plait to form a tie, and thread through eyelets.

Sian Brown

After doing a Fashion/ Textiles BA, Sian worked for companies in London supplying to high street retailers on machine knits. She became interested in handknits and have designed these since, working for magazines, publishers and yarn companies. Sian has a book, *The Knitted Home*, and have designed on several others. Visit her website at **sianbrown.com**.

Weekender hat

**Knit in rounds to discover this easy, casual, yet elegant style —
perfect for protecting against cold weather**

Difficulty ★★☆☆☆

Skills needed

Increasing
Decreasing
Lace stitches
Knitting in rounds
Specialist cast-on

Finished measurements

To fit sizes: 18 (21, 23) in
                   45.75 (53.5, 58.5) cm
Finished size: 14.75 (17.25, 19.75) in
                   37 (43, 49.25) cm

Yarn

For this project we have used one ball of
Rowan Cocoon yarn, which is made up
of 80 per cent Merino, 20 per cent Kid
Mohair. You will need a total of 76 (94,
114) metres, 83 (103, 125) yards.

Tension (Gauge)

14 sts and 20 rows = 10cm (4in) in
stocking (stockinette) stitch using 6mm
(US 10) needles.

Needles

5.5mm (US 9) circular needle, 40cm
(16in) long
6mm (US 10) circular needle, 40cm
(16in) long
6mm (US 10) DPNs

Other supplies

1 stitch marker
Tapestry needle

Woolly Wormhead

Woolly is a Hat Architect.
With a flair for unusual
construction, Woolly is
a designer whose patterns are
celebrated by knitters all over the world.
www.woollywormhead.com.

Weekender hat

Pattern recommends the Alternate Cable cast-on method — any suitable rib cast-on method will work.

Using 5.5mm needles and alternate cable cast-on method, cast (bind) on 48 (56, 64) sts.

Join in the round, being careful not to twist sts.

Place stitch marker to indicate start of round.

Brim

Rnd 1: *K1, P1; rep from * to end.
Repeat this round for 5cm (2in) (or desired length).
Inc Rnd: *K2, M1; rep from * to end. (72, 84, 96 sts.)

Body

Change to 6mm (US 10) needles for the remainder of the hat, changing to the DPNs for the crown when the hat becomes too small to work comfortably on the circular needle.

Rnd 1: *Yo, K2tog; rep from * to end.

Repeat this round to form the bias eyelet rib pattern until the body of the hat (excluding the brim) measures 9.5 (10.25, 10.75) cm, 3.75 (4, 4.25) in.

Crown

Foundation Rnd: Knit all sts.
45.75cm (18in) size jump to Rnd 5, 53.5cm (21in) size jump to Rnd 3, 58.5cm (23in) size start at Rnd 1, decreasing on every round as follows:

Rnd 1: *K14, ssk; rep from * to end. (90 sts.)
Rnd 2: *K13, ssk; rep from * to end. (84 sts.)
Rnd 3: *K12, ssk; rep from * to end. (78 sts.)
Rnd 4: *K11, ssk; rep from * to end. (72 sts.)
Rnd 5: *K10, ssk; rep from * to end. (66 sts.)
Rnd 6: *K9, ssk; rep from * to end. (60 sts.)
Rnd 7: *K8, ssk; rep from * to end. (54 sts.)
Rnd 8: *K7, ssk; rep from * to end. (48 sts.)
Rnd 9: *K6, ssk; rep from * to end. (42 sts.)
Rnd 10: *K5, ssk; rep from * to end. (36 sts.)
Rnd 11: *K4, ssk; rep from * to end. (30 sts.)
Rnd 12: *K3, ssk; rep from * to end. (24 sts.)
Rnd 13: *K2, ssk; rep from * to end. (18 sts.)
Rnd 14: *K1, ssk; rep from * to end. (12 sts.)
Rnd 15: *Ssk; rep from * to end. (6 sts.)
Break yarn and draw through remaining 6 sts. Tighten to close.

Making up

Weave in all ends. A gentle wash and blocking is required to help the decrease lines settle in and lay flat.

Basketweave fingerless mitts

Sometimes fingered gloves just aren't practical. Have a go at making some funky fingerless mitts th. will keep your hands warm but still enable you to carry out everyday tasks

Difficulty ★★☆☆☆

Skills needed
Increasing
Knitting in rows
Seaming

Finished measurements
Sizes approximate around palm or hand.
Small: 15cm (6 in)
Medium: 18cm (7 inches)
Large: 19 cm (7.5 inches)

Yarn
For this pattern you will need a 4 ply yarn.
For this example, Wendy Roam Fusion in
Force (above) and Heath (right) was used.

You will need one ball.

Tension (Gauge)
37 sts and 52 rows = 10 cm (4 ins) over
basket weave stitch

Needles
2¾ mm (US 2) knitting needles

Other supplies
Safety pin to hold 20 sts.

Construction notes
There is a lot of counting involved in
the pattern. When reaching the thumb,
remember to count the 35 stitches across
before breaking the basket weave in order

to do the thumb stitches.
   Be wary when following the 'patt to end'
in order to match it up to continue the
basketweave effect.

Basketweave fingerless mitts

Using 2¾ mm needles, cast (bind) on 57 (65, 73) sts.

Ribbed cuff

1st Row: K3, P2, * K2, P2 rep from * to end.
2nd Row: * K2, P2, rep from * to last st, P1
These two rows form rib. Continue in rib as set until work measures 7cm, 2¾ ins.

Commence basket weave pattern

Row 1: (rs) K1, * K2, P6, rep from * to end.
Row 2: (ws) * K6, P2, rep from * to last st, P1.
Row 3: As row 1.
Row 4: Purl.
Row 5: P5, * K2, P6, rep from * to last 4 stitches, K2, P2.
Row 6: K2, P2, *K6, P2, rep from * to last 5 sts, K5.
Row 7: As row 5.
Row 8: Purl.
These rows form basket weave pattern. Work rows 1 to 8 once and then work rows 1 to 4.

Thumb

Row 13: Keeping basket weave pattern correct, and starting from 5th row of pattern, patt 28 (32, 36) sts, M1, K2, M1, patt to end.
Row 14: Patt 27 (31, 35) sts, P4, patt to end.
Row 15: Patt 28 (32, 36) sts, K4, patt to end.
Row 16: Patt 27 (31, 35) sts, M1 pwise, P4, M1 pwise, patt to end.
Row 17: Patt 28 (32, 36) sts, K6, patt to end.
Row 18: Patt 27 (31, 35) sts, P6, patt to end.
Row 19: Patt 28 (32, 36) sts, M1, K6, M1, patt to end.
Row 20: Patt 27 (31, 35) sts, P8, patt to end.
Row 21: Patt 28 (32, 36) sts, K8, patt to end.
Row 22: Patt 27 (31, 35) sts, M1 pwise, P8, M1 pwise, patt to end.
Row 23: Patt 28 (32, 36) sts, K10, patt to end.
Row 24: Patt 27 (31, 35) sts, P10, patt to end.
Row 25: Patt 28 (32, 36) sts, M1, K10, M1,

patt to end.
Row 26: Patt 27 (31, 35) sts, P12, patt to end.
Row 27: Patt 28 (32, 36) sts, K12, patt to end.
Row 28: Patt 27 (31, 35) sts, M1 pwise, P12, M1 pwise, patt to end.
Row 29: Patt 28 (32, 36) sts, K14, patt to end.
Row 30: Patt 27 (31, 35) sts, P14, patt to end.
Row 31: Patt 28 (32, 36) sts, M1, K14, M1, patt to end.
Row 32: Patt 27 (31, 35) sts, P16, patt to end.
Row 33: Patt 28 (32, 36) sts, K16, patt to end.
Row 34: Patt 27 (31, 35) sts, M1 pwise, P16, M1 pwise, patt to end.
Row 35: Patt 28 (32, 36) sts, K18, patt to end.
Row 36: Patt 27 (31, 35) sts, P18, patt to end.
Row 37: Patt 28 (32, 36) sts, M1, K18, M1, patt to end.
Row 38: Patt 27 (31, 35) sts, P20, patt to end.
Row 39: Patt 28 (32, 36) sts, K20, patt to end.

1st size only

Row 40: Patt 27 (31, 35) sts, slip next 20 sts onto a safety pin, cast (bind) on 2 sts, patt to end.

2nd and 3rd sizes only

Row 40: Patt (31, 35) sts, M1 pwise, P20, M1 pwise, patt to end.
Row 41: Patt (32, 36) sts, K22, patt to end.
Row 42: Patt (31, 35) sts, M1 pwise, P22, M1 pwise, patt to end.
Row 43: Patt (32, 36) sts, K 24, patt to end.
Row 44: Patt (31, 35) sts, slip next 24 sts onto a safety pin, cast (bind) on 2 sts, patt to end.

All sizes

Work 16 (18, 20) more rows in basket weave pattern over all 57 (65, 73) sts on needle.
  Work 8 rows in rib, as worked for ribbed cuff.
Cast (bind) off.

Thumb

Return to sts left on safety pin, rejoin yarn with wrong side facing and P across 20 (24, 24) sts, pick up and P 4 sts over the 2 cast (bind) on sts.
Next Row: K1, M1, K1, P2, * K2, P2, rep from * to end.
Next Row: * K2, P2, rep from * to last st, P1.
Next Row: K3, P2, *K2, P2, rep from * to end.
Rep last 2 rows 4 times more, and then cast (bind) off in rib.

Making up

Join side seam and thumb seam by top sewing
Repeat for the other mitt.

Staggered beanie

Create this fantastic beanie with a staggered block pattern by knitting in the round, perfect as a gift for anyone

Difficulty ★★☆☆☆

Skills needed
Increasing
Decreasing
Knitting in rounds

Finished measurements
To fit sizes: 15 (18, 20, 22, 24) in
38 (45.75, 50.75, 56, 61) cm

Finished size: 13 (15.25, 17.5, 19.75, 21.75) in
33.25 (38.75, 44.25, 50, 55.5) cm

Yarn
For this project you will need a DK yarn. In this example, Debbie Bliss Blue Faces Leicester DK was used in Chestnut. You will need 45 (60, 78, 98, 120) m/49 (66, 85, 107, 131) yd.

Tension (Gauge)
22 sts and 35 rounds = 10cm (4in) in stocking (stockinette) stitch

Needles
3.25mm (US 3) circular needle, 40cm (16in) long
3.25mm (US 3) DPNs

Other supplies
1 stitch marker
Tapestry needle

Woolly Wormhead
Woolly is a Hat Architect. With a flair for unusual construction, Woolly is a designer whose patterns are celebrated by knitters all over the world.
www.woollywormhead.com.

Staggered beanie

Using cast (bind) on method of your choice, cast (bind) on 72 (84, 96, 108, 120) sts onto the circular needle. Join in the round, being careful not to twist sts. Place stitch marker to indicate start of round.

Brim
Rnd 1: *K3, P3; repeat from * to end
Repeat this round until brim measures 1 (1.25, 1.5, 1.75, 2) in/2.5 (3.25, 3.75, 4.5, 5) cm.

Body
Rnd 1: *K3, P9; repeat from * to end
Repeat this round for a further 1 (1.25, 1.5, 1.75, 2) in/2.5 (3.25, 3.75, 4.5, 5) cm until work measures 2 (2.5, 3, 3.5, 4) in/5 (6.25, 7.5, 9, 10.25) cm from cast (bind)-on edge. Work as follows:
Next rnd: Purl all sts
Repeat this round, forming reverse stocking (stockinette) stitch, for a further 1.5in/3.75cm until work measures 3.5 (4, 4.5, 5, 5.5) in/9 (10.25, 11.5, 12.75, 14) cm from cast (bind)-on edge.

Crown preparation
18in size only: *p2tog, P19; repeat from * to end. 80 sts.
22in size only: *P12, p2tog, P13; repeat from * to end. 104 sts.

Crown
15in/38cm size jump to Rnd 13; 18in/45cm size jump to Rnd 11; 20in/50.75cm size jump to Rnd 7; 22in/56cm size jump to Rnd 5; 24in/61cm size start at Rnd 1.

As you work through these instructions, as the hat gets too small to work comfortably on the circular needle, change to the DPNs.
Rnd 1: *(ssp, P26, p2tog); repeat from * to end. 112 sts.
Rnd 2 & all even rounds: Purl all sts
Rnd 3: P12, p2tog, (ssp, P24, p2tog) 3 times, ssp, P12. 104 sts.
Rnd 5: *(ssp, P22, p2tog); repeat from * to end. 96 sts.
Rnd 7: P10, p2tog, (ssp, P20, p2tog) 3 times, ssp, P10/ 88 sts.
Rnd 9: *(ssp, P18, p2tog); repeat from * to end. 80 sts.
Rnd 11: P8, p2tog, (ssp, P16, p2tog) 3 times, ssp, P8/ 72 sts.
Rnd 13: *(ssp, P14, p2tog); repeat from * to end. 64 sts.
Rnd 15: P6, p2tog, (ssp, P12, p2tog) 3 times, ssp, P6. 56 sts.
Rnd 17: *(ssp, P10, p2tog); repeat from * to end. 48 sts.
Rnd 19: P4, p2tog, (ssp, P8, p2tog) 3 times, ssp, P4. 40 sts.
Rnd 21: *(ssp, P6, p2tog); repeat from * to end. 32 sts.
Rnd 23: P2, p2tog, (ssp, P4, p2tog) 3 times, ssp, P2. 24 sts.
Rnd 25: *(ssp, P2, p2tog); repeat from * to end. 16 sts.
Rnd 27: *(p2tog, ssp); repeat from * to end. 8 sts.
Break yarn and draw through remaining 8 sts, tighten to close.

Making up
Weave in all ends. A gentle wash and blocking is required to help the decreases settle in and lay flat.

2x3 rib scarf

Now that you have mastered rib stitch, have a go at this quick to knit scarf. Perfect to keep anyone cosy, as the 2x3 rib stitch causes ripples in the fabric, which will hold in warm air

Difficulty ★☆☆☆☆

Skills needed
Knitting in rows
Rib stitches
Cast (bind) off in rib

Finished measurements
140cm (55in) x 18cm (7in)

Yarn
For this project you will need an Aran weight yarn. In this example we have used Sirdar Hayfield Bonus Aran in Denim. You will need approximately 420m (459yd).

Tension (Gauge)
28sts and 22 rows = 10cm (4in) in 2x3 rib stitch using 5mm (US 8) needles.

Needles
5mm (US 8) needles

Other supplies
Tapestry needle

2x3 rib scarf
Cast on 50 sts using 5mm needles
Row 1: *K3, P2; rep from * to end.
Row 2: *K2, P2; rep from * to end.
These 2 rows form 2x3 rib pattern.
Continue in pattern until your knitting measures 140cm (55in), or your desired length, from the cast (bind) on edge.
   Cast (bind) off.

Making up
Darn in ends and gently block.

Did you know?
You can use different combinations of knit and purl stitches to create a different looking rib pattern. A 2x2 rib is common for a good stretchy cuff on knitted hats.

Lou Butt

Lou has been designing knitwear for print and independently for over ten years. She started knitting aged seven when her mum owned a yarn shop in Cornwall, and hasn't put her needles down since. Find her work in Knitted Sock Sensations, Complete Knitting and Socks Rock.

Cosy welly socks

Whether you're on a dog walk, splashing in puddles or pottering in the garden, keep your feet cosy with these thick welly socks

Difficulty ★★★★☆

Skills needed

Decreasing
Cable
Pick up & knit
Knitting in rounds
Kitchener stitch
Turning a heel

Finished measurements

They are thick, so if your wellies are snug, make them a little shorter. The measurements in this pattern are designed to fit a women's size 6 foot of average width. The length of foot can be adjusted for a better fit; see notes in the pattern.

Yarn

For this pattern you will require a super chunky yarn to keep your toes nice and toasty. In this example Wendy Serenity Super Chunky has been used, which is made up of 10 per cent wool, 20 per cent alpaca and 70 per cent acrylic. The shade used is 1711 Peony. You will need 2 balls.

Tension (Gauge)

10 stitches and 14 rounds = 10cm (4in) in stocking stitch

Needles

10mm (US 15) 4x double pointed needles

Lou Butt

Lou has been designing knitwear for print and independently for over ten years. She started knitting aged seven when her mum owned a yarn shop in Cornwall, and hasn't put her needles down since. Find her work in Knitted Sock Sensations, Complete Knitting and Socks Rock.

Other supplies
1 stitch marker
Cable needle
Tapestry needle

Construction notes
Both socks are worked in the same way, except for the cable stitch. On one sock the cable is turned left, on the other the cable is turned right.

Special st instructions:
C4B: Slip the next 2 sts onto your cable needle and hold at *back* of work, K the next 2 sts on the left-hand needle, then K the sts from the cable needle.
C4F: Slip the next 2 sts onto your cable needle and hold at *front* of work, K the next 2 sts on the left-hand needle, then K the sts from the cable needle.

Right sock cable pattern
Worked over 11 sts, in the round
Rnds 1 & 2: K3, P2, K4, P2.
Rnd 3: K3, P2, C4B, P2.
Rnd 4: K3, P2, K4, P2.

Left sock cable pattern
Worked over 11 sts, in the round
Rnds 1 & 2: K3, P2, K4, P2.
Rnd 3: K3, P2, C4F, P2.
Rnd 4: K3, P2, K4, P2.

Cosy welly socks
Cast 30 sts onto a single needle.
　Arrange stitches evenly over 3 needles being careful not to twist the stitches.
　Slip the first st of the left-hand needle, onto the right needle, next lift the first st on the right needle over the top of the st you just slipped and place it on the left-hand needle.
　This will be the first st you work.
　Place a stitch marker between stitches 1 and 2 to denote the beginning of the round.
Rnd 1 (establish ribbing): (K1, P1) to end.
Rep rnd 1 8 more times.
Next rnd (establish cable pattern): Work appropriate Cable pattern over first 11 sts of round, K to end.

Work 8 rounds in pattern as set, until 2 full repeats of the Cable pattern have been worked.
Next rnd (dec): Work Cable pattern as set, K2, K2tog, K to last 2 sts, K2tog. (28 sts.)
Work 7 rounds even as set.
Next rnd (dec): Work Cable pattern as set, K1, K2tog, K to last 2 sts, K2tog. (26 sts.)

Continue even in pattern until piece from cast-on edge measures 43cm (17in), ending with Rnd 4 of the cable pattern.

Divide for heel
Arrange your stitches so that there are 14 on the first needle of the round. The heel is worked on these stitches only.
Row 1 (RS): Sl1, K2, P2, K4, P2, K3. Turn.
Row 2 (WS): Sl1, P2, K2, P4, K2, P3. Turn.
Repeat these 2 rows twice more.

Turn heel
Row 1 (RS): Sl1, K7, SSK, K1. Turn.
Row 2 (WS): Sl 1, P3, P2tog, P1. Turn.
Row 3: Sl 1, K4, SSK, K1. Turn.
Row 4: Sl 1, P5, P2tog, P1. Turn.
Row 5: Sl 1, K6, SSK. Turn.
Row 6: Sl 1, P6, P2tog. Turn. 8 sts rem on heel.
Rnd 1 (gusset setup):
Needle 1: Knit 8 heel sts, then pick up and knit 4 sts along first side of heel, using the slipped sts as a guide.

Needle 2: Knit all 12 sts.
Needle 3: Pick up and knit 4 sts along second side of heel flap using the slipped sts as a guide, then K4 sts from the first needle.
Gusset rnd 2:
Needle 1: K to last 3 sts, k2tog, K1.
Needle 2: K.
Needle 3: K1, SSK, k to end of needle. (2 sts decreased)
Gusset rnd 3: Knit all sts.
Repeat gusset round 2 once more. 24 sts rem.
Now knit every round until work from heel to needles measures 19cm (7.5in), or 5cm (2in) short of full foot length.

Shape toe
Rnd 1:
Needle 1: K to last 3 sts, K2tog, K1.
Needle 2: K1, SSK, K to last 3 sts, K2tog, K1.
Needle 3: K1, SSK, K to end of needle. (4 sts decreased.)
Rnd 2: Knit.
Rep Rnd 1 and 2 once more. 16 sts. Work Rnd 1 twice. (8 sts)
Knit the sts from needle 1 onto needle 3.
With right side facing, graft the toe using a kitchener stitch.

Making up
Darn in ends.

Nordic winter hat

Keep yourself warm when the temperatures begin to drop with this fun Nordic-style hat

Difficulty ★★★☆☆

Skills needed
Decreasing
Colourwork (stranded)
Knitting in rounds
Working from a chart

Finished measurements
One size fits most people
Circumference: 55cm (22in)
Length: 34cm (13.5in)

Yarn
For this pattern you will need a super chunky yarn. In this example Drops Eskimo
has been used. You will need approximately 100m (108 yd).
Colour 1: Red; 2 x balls
Colour 2: White; 1 x ball
Colour 3: Grey; 1 x ball

Tension (Gauge)
13 stitches and 16 rounds = 10cm (4in) in stocking (stockinette) stitch

Needles
8mm (US 11) 40cm (16in) circular needle
8mm (US 11) DPNs

Other supplies
1 stitch marker
Tapestry needle

Nordic winter hat
With contrast colour 2, cast (bind) on 72 stitches on circular needles. Join to work in the round and take care so you don't to twist the cast (bind)on edge as you do so. Place a stitch marker in order to indicate the beginning of the round
Work rib (K2, P2) for 4 rounds.
Start working the chart, joining main colour on round 1 of chart and joining contrast colour 1 on round 8 of chart.

When you have finished working the chart, knit 1 round in main colour, and continue in main colour as follows:
Change to double-pointed needles when the stitches do not go easily around the needle.
Rnd 1 (dec): *K7, k2tog* around — 64 sts.
Rnd 2: K
Rnd 3 (dec): *K2, k2tog* around — 48 sts.
Rnd 4: K
Rnd 5 (dec): *K1, k2tog* around — 32 sts.
Cut the yarn about 40cm (16in) from the work.
Pass the yarn through the live stitches on the needles.
Pass the thread at the top through the hole in the middle and turn the hat inside out. Pull the loose end tight (make sure you don't pull so hard you break it!).
With a tapestry needle, secure the end and make a few stitches to cover up the hole that is left at the top

Making up
Weave in loose ends.
With an iron set on Wool and the steam function on, gently press the hat.

Eline Oftedal

Eline is a Norwegian knitting designer who lives and works in Oslo. She has a deep affinity for traditional Scandinavian knitting, and her heritage can often be seen in her designs. She sells individual patterns online and teaches classes in knitting in several countries. You can see more from Eline at **byeline.no**.

Key: ☐ White　▨ Light grey　■ Red

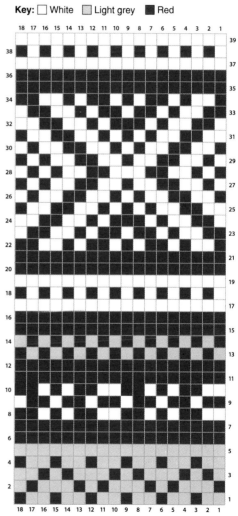

Owl hat and mitts

Learn how to make these adorable items for children, just perfect for a bright and colourful gift on a birthday or as a baby shower present

Difficulty ★★☆☆☆

Skills needed
Increasing
Decreasing
Knitting in rows

Finished measurements
Owl Hat:
Width around head (when slightly stretched)

33	35.5	38	41	43	*cm*
13	14	15	16	17	*ins*

Mitts to fit corresponding age:
Age (approximate)

Prem 0	6	12	24	*months*

Yarn
For this pattern you shall require DK yarn. In the example, Peter Pan DK was used in Blue Jeans, Jade and White, kindly supplied by Thomas B Ramsden.
Colour 1: Blue Jeans; 1 x ball
Colour 2: Jade; 1 x ball
Colour 3: White; 1 x ball

Tension (Gauge)
24 sts and 32 rows = 10cm (4in) in stocking (stockinette) stitch on 4mm needles

Needles
2 - 3¼mm (US 3)

Other supplies
Tapestry needle

Thomas B Ramsden
This pattern was kindly supplied by Thomas B Ramsden, a family business who are the suppliers of Wendys and Peter Pan, two of the biggest brands of yarn in the UK. You can find them at **www.tbramsden.co.uk**.

Hat

Using 3¼mm needles and col 2, cast (bind) on 73 (79, 85, 91, 97) sts.

Row 1: K1, * P1, K1, rept from * to end.
Row 2: P1, * K1, P1, rept from * to end.

These two rows form rib, repeat 1st and 2nd row three times more.

Change to 4mm needles and join in A. Now, working in st st throughout, and commencing with a K row, work 2 rows in col 1 then 2 rows in col 2.

Last 4 rows set stripe pattern, repeat these 4 rows 3 (3, 4, 5, 5) times more. Break off col 2, and continue in col 1 only.

Continue in st st until hat measures 12 (12, 13, 14, 14)cm, 4¾ (4¾, 5¼, 5½, 5½) ins from cast (bind)-on edge ending on a P row.

Cast (bind) off.

Eyes

Using 4mm needles and col 3, cast (bind) on 3 sts.

Row 1: [Inc in next st], rept in each st to end. 6 sts.
Row 2: [Inc in next st], rept in each st to end. 12 sts.
Row 3: K1, * inc in next st , K1 rept from * to last st, K1. 17 sts.
Row 4: K1, * inc in next st , K1 rept from * to end. 25 sts.

Cast (bind) off.

Join row end edges, work will then form a circle.

Inner eyes (Make 2)

Using 4mm needles and col 2, cast (bind) on 5 sts.

Row 1: Sl 1, P3, sl 1.
Row 2: K5
Row 3: Sl 1, P3, sl 1
Row 4: K5

Cast (bind) off pwise.

Run a gathering stitch around outer edge, and gather up to form a small berry shape.

Beak

Using 4mm needles and col 2, cast (bind) on 2 sts.

Row 1: Purl.
Row 2: K1, m1, K1.
Row 3: P3.

Row 4: K1, m1, K1, m1, K1.
Row 5: P5.

Cast (bind) off.

Making up

Using the photograph as a guide, and placing the beak at centre of work, attach eyes and beak as shown.

Fold in side edges of hat so that they meet at centre back. Join back seam and top seam by top sewing.

Mitts

Using 4mm needles and col 1, cast (bind) on 26(26, 28, 28, 30) sts.

Row 1: * K1, P1, rept from * to end
Repeat this row 5 times more.

Row 7: (Make eyelet holes) K1, * yo, K2tog, rept from * to last st, K1.
Next row: Purl to end.

Continue in st st for a further 20 (22, 24, 28, 30) rows, ending with a purl row.

Cast (bind) off loosely.

Eyes (Make 2)

Using 4mm needles and col 3, cast (bind) on 3 sts.

Row 1: [Inc in next st], rept in each st to end. 6 sts.
Row 2: [Inc in next st], rept in each st to end. 12sts.
Row 3: K1, * inc in next st, K1 rept from * to last st, K1. (18sts)

Cast (bind) off.

Join row end edges, work will then form a circle.

Inner eyes (Make 2)

Work as given for inner eyes of hat.

Beak

Work as given for beak of hat.

Making up

Fold mitten in half, so the seam is at one side.

Using the photograph as a guide, attach eyes and beak as shown.

Join side and top seam by top sewing.

Using col 2 and col 3, make a twisted cord and thread through eyelet holes.

Parlour cat

Make your very own feline friend and apply your knitting skills to this cuddly creation that will make the perfect gift for any animal lover

Difficulty ★★★★★

Skills needed
Increasing
Decreasing
Pick up & knit
Knitting in rounds
Wrap and turn (short rows)

Finished measurements
25cm (10in) long

Yarn
For this project you will need a DK yarn. In the example, Red Heart Super Saver was used. You shall need a total of 155m (170yd) in your chosen colour.

Tension (Gauge)
22 sts and 30 rounds = 10cm (4in) in st st
Note that tension is not very important with toys. Changing yarn weight or needle size will make your finished object smaller or larger. You should work the fabric more densely than you would for a scarf or a garment, so that it holds the stuffing in.

Needles
3.5mm (US 4) DPNs

Other supplies
2 stitch markers
Buttons for eyes (optional)
Length of scrap yarn
Tapestry needle
Stuffing

Sara Elizabeth Kellner
Sara Elizabeth Kellner is a knitting designer who combines her love of art, animals, and children to create charming and whimsical toy patterns. See more from Sara on her website: **www.rabbitholeknits.com**.

Did you know?
Hazel Tindall currently holds the title of World's Fastest Knitter, completing 262 stitches in 3 minutes.

Parlour cat
Body
Cast (bind) on 52 sts onto a single needle. Distribute across 3 DPNs, placing 18 stitches on the first two needles, and 16 on the third, and join for working in the round.

Rounds 1-2: Knit.
Round 3: K1, m1, K2, m1, K to last 3 sts, m1, K2, m1, K1. (4 sts increased.)
Round 4-7: Knit
Round 8-17: Repeat rounds 2-7 twice more. (64 sts.)
Round 18: K1, m1, K2, m1, K2, m1, K to last 5 sts, m1, K2, m1, K2, m1, K1. (6 sts increased).
Rounds 19-22: Knit.
Round 23-27: Repeat rounds 18-22 once more.
Round 28: Repeat round 18. (82 sts.)
Rounds 29-44: Knit.

Measure off about 25 yards of yarn for finishing the rear and tail later and then cut. Thread a darning needle with a piece of scrap yarn and slip all of the live sts onto it.

Chest
Stitches are now picked up in the original cast (bind) on sts to form the cat's chest. Count 10 sts to the left of the first cast (bind) on st, rejoin yarn and pick up and knit 15 sts in the cast on edge with the first needle; using a second needle, pick up and knit the following 15 sts.

Purl back across all sts on the second DPNs only. This will leave your working yarn in between the first and second DPNs, and you are ready to work the short rows.

Short rows are now worked back and forth across these two DPNs:
Row 1: K3, w&t,
Row 2 (WS): P6, w&t,
Row 3: K7, w&t,
Row 4: P8, w&t,
Row 5: K9, w&t,
Row 6: P10, w&t,
Row 7: K11, w&t,
Row 8: P12, w&t,

Continue like this, working one more st before the turn each row, until all but four sts on each end have been worked (3 sts unwrapped on each side). You will end with a Purl row.

Cut yarn

Head
Additional sts are now picked up between the end of the second DPN and beginning of the first. Rejoin yarn and with your third DPN, pick up 22 sts, one in each of the remaining cast (bind) on sts. (52 sts.)
Round 1: Knit.
Round 2: k2tog, K21, ssk, K1, k2tog, K to last 2 sts, ssk. (48 sts.)
Round 3: k2tog, K19, ssk, K1, k2tog, K to last 2 sts, ssk. (44 sts.)
Rounds 4-5: Knit.
Round 6: k2tog, K17, ssk, K1, k2tog, K to last 2 sts, ssk. (40 sts.)
Rounds 7-8: Knit.
Round 9: K1, m1, K17, m1, K3, m1, K to last 2 sts, m1, K2. (44 sts.)
Rounds 10-11: Knit.
Round 12: K1, m1, K19, m1, K3, m1, K to

last 2 sts, m1, K2. (48 sts.)

Rounds 13-14: Knit.

Round 15: K1, m1, K21, m1, K3, m1, K to last 2 sts, m1, K2. (52 sts.)

Rounds 16-17: Knit.

Round 18: K1, m1, K23, m1, K3, m1, K to last 2 sts, m1, K2. (56 sts.)

Rounds 19-20: Knit.

Round 21: K1, k2tog, K22, ssk, K2, k2tog, K to last 3 sts, ssk, K1. (52 sts.)

Rounds 22-23: Knit.

Round 24: K1, k2tog, K20, ssk, K2, k2tog, K to last 3 sts, ssk, K1. (48 sts.)

Rounds 25-26: Knit.

Round 27: K1, k2tog, K18, ssk, K2, k2tog, K to last 3 sts, SSK, K1. (44 sts.)

Rounds 28-29: Knit.

Slip the first 7 sts onto your working DPN without knitting them. Thread a darning needle with a piece of scrap yarn, and slip the next 30 sts onto it for working later. You now have 14 sts remaining on 2 DPNs. Transfer some of them to a third DPN for working in the round. With RS facing, rejoin yarn at the first original st on the outer right side of the head.

Rounds 1-3: Knit.

Round 4: ssk, K3, k2tog, ssk, K3, k2tog.

(10 sts.)

Round 5-6: Knit.

Round 7: ssk, K1, k2tog, ssk, K1, k2tog. (6 sts.)

Round 8: Knit.

Cut yarn and thread through a darning needle; thread yarn through remaining sts and pull tight to close. Insert needle down through center of ear and secure to inside.

Place the next 8 sts from scrap yarn at the front of the head onto a DPN. Place last 8 sts from the scrap yarn at the back of the head onto a 2nd DPN. Using Kitchener stitch, graft these 16 sts together to form the area between the ears. Arrange the 14 remaining live sts

onto 3 DPNs. The first stitch should be the innermost stitch on the right side of the ear. Repeat all rounds (1-8) for this ear as with the first one.

Sew up any holes, weave in any loose ends, and stuff the head and front half of body. Be sure to stuff the entire chest area very firmly. This will ensure the proper posture for your Parlour Cat.

Rear and tail

Return the 82 held sts from the scrap yarn back onto 3 DPNs.

Round 1: (K7, k2tog) 4 times, .K10, (K7, k2tog) 4 times. (74 sts.)

Round 2: Knit.

Round 3: (K6, k2tog) 4 times, K10, (K6,

k2tog) 4 times. (66 sts.)
Round 4: Knit.
Round 5: (K5, k2tog) 4 times, K10, (K5, k2tog) 4 times. (58 sts.)
Round 6: Knit.
Round 7: (K4, k2tog) 4 times, K10, (K4, k2tog) 4 times. (50 sts.)
Round 8: Knit.
Round 9: (K3, k2tog) 4 times, K10, (K3, k2tog) 4 times. (42 sts.)
Round 10: Knit.
Round 11: (K2, k2tog) 4 times, K10, (K2, k2tog) 4 times. (34 sts.)
Round 12: Knit.
Round 13: (K1, k2tog) 4 times, K10, (K1, k2tog) 4 times. (26 sts.)
Round 14: Knit.
Round 15: k2tog 4 times, K10, k2tog 4 times. (18 sts.)
The 18 remaining sts will form the tail.

Finish stuffing the cat's body. Knit all sts for 3 inches, working a k2tog at the start of the round every inch or so, until 15 sts rem. Knit all 15 sts for approximately 12.5cm (5in).
Next round: k2tog, k to end of round.
Following round: Knit.
Repeat the last 2 rounds twice more. (12 sts)
    Knit all sts for 1 inch. Cut yarn, thread through remaining live sts. Stuff tail, pull tightly closed, and secure. Hold the tail alongside of the body and seam together at bottom.

Front legs
Cast on 15 sts onto a single needle. Distribute across 3 DPNs, placing 5 on each needle, and join for working in the round. Knit all sts for 12.5cm (5 in).
    Cut yarn, thread through live sts, pull tightly closed and secure. Stuff all but about 1 inch at open end.
    Fold the closed end of paw inward and stitch to hold in place. Seam leg to bottom of cat's body.

Finishing
Create the face
Eyes, nose, mouth and whiskers can be embroidered, painted or appliqueed. Make your Parlour Cat as unique as you like!

Plumley the penguin

Work with different colours to make this bright and fun design — a cute addition to any home

Difficulty ★★★★☆

Skills needed

Increasing
Decreasing
Colourwork (stranded)
Colourwork (intarsia)
Knitting in rows
Working from a chart
Seaming

Finished measurements

Height (excluding hat): approximately 19cm (7.5in)
Width (around widest part of penguin): 33.5cm (17in)
Width (around head): 21.5cm (8.5in)

Yarn

For this pattern you will need a DK yarn. In the example, Hayfield Bonus DK was used in Black, Cream, Sunflower and Signal red.
Colour 1: Black; 1 x ball
Colour 2: Cream; 1 x ball
Colour 3: Sunflower; 1 x ball
Colour 4: Signal red; 1 x ball

Tension (Gauge)

Tension is not important as it's a toy.

Needles

3.5mm (US 4) needles

Other supplies

Wool needle
2 x 8mm toy safety eyes (note: for safety reasons, use yarn eyes for under 3's)

Lynne Rowe

Lynne is a knitting and crochet designer, writer and tutor from Cheshire. Her aim is to encourage as many people as possible to knit and crochet. To read more about Lynne, visit her website at **lynnerowe.weebly.com**.

Pattern notes

When working the stranded colourwork rows in col 3 (Rows 5, 9, 13, 17, 21, 25, 29), cut yarn after each row, leaving a 15cm (6in) tail end for weaving in later. Split black into 2 balls ready for the intarsia rows on body and head. Always twist yarns at colour change to avoid making holes.

Plumley the penguin

Penguin base

Using col 1, cast (bind) on 10 sts.

Row 1 (WS): Purl.

Row 2 (RS): kfb in every st. (20 sts.)

Row 3 and every alternate row: Purl.

Row 4: [K1, kfb] to end. (30 sts.)

Row 6: [K2, kfb] to end. (40 sts.)

Row 8: [K3, kfb] to end. (50 sts.)

Row 10: [K4, kfb] to end. (60 sts.)

Rows 12-13: Knit.

Penguin body

The penguin body uses intarsia, working a section of cream (col 2) in the centre of the two col 1 sections. Use a separate ball of col 1 for each section and always twist yarns at colour change on every row to avoid holes.

Rows 5, 9, 13, 17, 21, 25 and 29 also used stranded colourwork. See the 'Pattern notes' section.

Row 1 (RS): K25 with col 1, K9 with col 2, K26 with col 1.

Row 2: P25 with col 1, P11 with col 2, P24 with col 1.

Row 3: K23 with col 1, K13 with col 2, K24 with col 1.

Row 4: P23 with col 1, P15 with col 2, P22 with col 1.

Row 5: With col 1 [K4, m1] 5 times, K2, [K1 with col 2, K1 with col 3] 7 times, K1 with col 2, with col 1 K3, [m1, K4] 5 times. (70 sts.)

Rows 6, 8, 10, 12: P28 with col 1, P15 with col 2, P27 with col 1.

Row 7: K27 with col 1, K15 with col 2, K28 with col 1.

Row 9: K27 with col 1, K2 with col 2, [K1 with col 3, K1 with col 2] 6 times, K1 with col 2, K28 with col 1.

Row 11: Rep Row 7

Row 13: With col 1 K2, [k2tog, K3] 5 times, [K1 with col 2, K1 with col 3] 7

times, K1 with col 2, with col 1 [K3, k2tog] 5 times, K3. (60 sts.)

Rows 14, 16, 18, 20: P23 with col 1, P15 with col 2, P22 with col 1.

Row 15: K22 with col 1, K15 with col 2, K23 with col 1.

Row 17: K22 with col 1, K2 with col 2, [K1 with col 3, K1 with col 2] 6 times, K1 with col 2, K23 with col 1.

Row 19: Rep Row 15.

Row 21: With col 1 K2, [k2tog, K2] 5 times, [K1 with col 2, K1 with col 3] 7 times, K1 with col 2, with col 1 [K2, k2tog] 5 times, K3. (50 sts.)

Rows 22, 24, 26, 28: P18 with col 1, P15 with col 2, P17 with col 1.

Row 23: K17 with col 1, K15 with col 2, K18 with col 1.

Row 25: K17 with col 1, K2 with col 2, [K1 with col 3, K1 with col 2] 6 times, K1 with

col 2, K18 with col 1.

Row 27: Rep Row 23.

Row 29: With col 1 [K2, k2tog] 4 times, K1, [K1 with col 2, K1 with col 3] 7 times, K1 with col 2, with col 1 [K2, k2tog] 4 times, K2. (42 sts.)

Row 30: P14 with col 1, P15 with col 2, P13 with col 1.

Row 31: K13 with col 1, K15 with col 2, K14 with col 1.

Row 32: Rep Row 30.

Row 33: K13 with col 1, with col 2 K2, skpo, K1, skpo, K1, k2tog, K1, k2tog, K2, K14 with col 1. (38 sts.)

Row 34: P14 with col 1, P11 with col 2, P13 with col 1.

Row 35: K13 with col 1, with col 2, K2, skpo, K3, k2tog, K2, K14 with col 1. (36 sts.)

Row 36: P14 with col 1, P9 with col 2, P13 with col 1.

Head

Row 37: K13 with col 1, K9 with col 2, K14 with col 1.

Row 38: P14 with col 1, P9 with col 2, P13 with col 1.

Rows 39-46: Rep Rows 37-38 4 more times.

Row 47: K14 with col 1, K7 with col 2, K15 with col 1.

Row 48: P16 with col 1, P5 with col 2, P15 with col 1. From here, continue with one ball of col 1 and cut all other yarns.

Rows 49-56: With col 1, starting with a K row, work in st st for 8 rows.

Row 57: K1, [K1, k2tog] to the last 2 sts, K2. (25 sts.)

Row 58: Purl.

Row 59: [K1, k2tog] to the last st, K1. (17 sts.)

Row 60: P1, [p2tog] to end. (9 sts.)

Cut yarn, leaving a long tail of approximately 45cm (18in) for sewing up. Using a darning needle, thread tail end through the 9 rem sts. Pull tight to gather and tie off yarn to secure gathers. Tie off and trim all other yarn ends (except for the long tail end, which you will use to sew the back seam.)

If you are using toy safety eyes, attach them now at approximately Row 45, leaving a gap of approximately 1.5cm (.5in) between the eyes. If the penguin is for a small child, stitch the eyes by hand, using black yarn. Use the long tail end of yarn to stitch the back seam of the penguin, until you reach the last row of the Penguin base. Fill the head and body with toy filling until nice and plump (note, the bottom half of the penguin back is wider than the top half, to make the roly-poly shape). Cont to stitch the base until you reach the cast (bind) on sts. Gather the cast (bind) on sts and pull tightly to close the hole. Tie off yarn and weave end into the penguin body.

Beak (Make 1)

Using col 3, cast (bind) on 10 sts.

Rows 1-2: Starting with a K row, work in st st for 2 rows.

Row 3: K1, skpo, K to last 3 sts, k2tog, K1.

(2 sts decreased).

Rows 4-6: Starting with a P row, work in st st for 3 rows.

Row 7: Rep Row 3. (6 sts.)

Row 8: Purl.

Row 9: K1, skpo, k2tog, K1. (4 sts.)

Row 10: Purl.

Row 11: k2tog twice. (2 sts.)

Rows 12-14: Starting with a P row, work in st st for 3 rows.

Row 15: kfb twice. (4 sts.)

Row 16: Purl.

Row 17: K1, m1, K to the last st, m1, K1.

(2 sts increased.)

Row 18: Purl.

Row 19: Rep Row 17. (8 sts.)

Rows 20-22: Starting with a P row, work in st st for 3 rows.

Row 23: Rep Row 17. (10 sts.)

Rows 24-26: Starting with a P row, work in st st for 3 rows.

Cast (bind) off (RS is facing). Fold beak in half with right sides facing and stitch the two sides, either by mattress stitch or by a simple whip stitch. Fill the beak lightly and stitch the top seam. Stitch the longest edge of the beak to the centre face of the penguin, below the eyes.

Feet (Make 2)

Using col 3, cast (bind) on 6 sts.

Rows 1-4: Knit.

Row 5: K1, kfb, K to the last 2 sts, kfb, K1. (2 sts increased.)

Rows 6-8: K all sts.

Rows 9-12: Rep Rows 5-8. (10 sts.)

Rows 13-16: Knit.

Row 17: K1, k2tog, K to the last 3 sts, k2tog, K1. (2 sts decreased.)

Rows 18-20: Knit.

Rows 21-24: Rep Rows 17-20 (6 sts.)

Cast (bind) off (RS is facing when you are casting (binding) off). Fold foot in half with WS together and RS facing outwards and stitch the two sides, either by mattress stitch or by a simple whip stitch. Fill the foot lightly and stitch the top seam. Stitch the shortest edge of the foot to the front of the penguin, at the edge of the base.

Flippers (Make 2)

Using col 1, cast (bind) on 6 sts (starting at the top of the flipper).

Rows 1-6: Starting with a K row, work in st st for 6 rows.

Row 7: K1, m1, K to the last st, m1, K1. (2 sts increased.)

Rows 8-12: Starting with a P row, work in st st for 5 rows.

Row 13-24: Rep Rows 7-12 twice more. (12 sts.)

Row 25: K1, skpo, K to last 3 sts, k2tog, K1. (2 sts decreased.)

Row 26: P

Row 27: Rep Row 25. (8 sts.)

Row 28: Purl.

Change to col 2.

Row 29: K1, m1, K to the last st, m1, K1. (2 sts increased.)

Row 30: Purl.

Row 31: Rep Row 29. (12 sts.)

Rows 32-36: Starting with a P row, work in st st for 5 rows.

Row 37: K1, skpo, K to the last 3 sts, k2tog K1. (2 sts decreased.)

Rows 38-42: Starting with a P row, work in st st for 5 rows.

Rows 43-54: Rep Rows 37-42 twice more (6 sts.)

Cast (bind) off (RS is facing when you are casting (binding) off). Fold flipper in half with right sides facing and stitch the two sides and top edge, using mattress stitch. Stitch the top edge of each flipper to

each side of the penguin body, just below the head.

Scarf

Using col 4 cast (bind) on 6 sts.
Rows 1-8: Starting with a K row, work in st st for 8 rows.
Join col 2, do not cut col 4.
Rows 9-116: Starting with a K row, work st st in stripes of 4 rows col 2 followed by 4 rows col 4, ending with 4 rows col 2.
Rows 117-124: In col 4, Rep Rows 1-8.
Cast (bind) off. The row ends of the scarf will naturally curl inwards. Tie off and trim all loose yarn ends. Place scarf around neck and stitch in place.

Hat

Using col 4, cast (bind) on 44 sts.
Rows 1-4: With col 4 [K1, P1] to the end.
Join col 2, do not cut col 4.
Row 5: With col 2, K3, [m1, K7] 5 times, m1, K6. (50 sts.)

Rows 6-8: With col 2, starting with a P row, work in st st for 3 rows.
Rows 9-10: With col 4, starting with a K row, work in st st for 2 rows.
Row 11: With col 4, [K3, k2tog] 10 times. (40 sts.)
Row 12: With col 4, P all sts.
Rows 13-14: With col 1, starting with a K row, work in st st for 2 rows.
Row 15: With col 2, [K2, k2tog] 10 times. (30 sts.)
Row 16: With col 2, P all sts.
Rows 17-18: With col 4, starting with a K row, work in st st for 2 rows.
Row 19: With col 4, [K1, k2tog] 10 times. (20 sts.)
Row 20: With col 4, P all sts.
Rows 21-22: With col 2, starting with a K row, work in st st for 2 rows.
Row 23: With col 2, k2tog 10 times. (10 sts.)
Row 24: With col 2, P all sts.
Rows 25-44: Starting with a K row, work

in st st for 20 rows, working in stripes of 4 rows in col 4 followed by 4 rows in col 2, ending with 4 rows in col 4.
Row 45: k2tog 5 times. (5 sts.)
Rows 46-48: Starting with a P row, work in st st for 3 rows.
Cut yarn and pull through final sts to secure, leaving a long tail for sewing up.

Making up

Stitch the hat seam using mattress stitch. Tie off all loose yarns ends and trim. Make a bobble as follows: Using col 4, wrap yarn around two fingers, approximately 40 times. Carefully remove yarn from fingers. Tie a separate length of yarn around the middle of the wrapped yarn and tie tightly. Cut folded ends of yarn then trim the bobble to make a nice round shape. Stitch the bobble to the top of the hat and stitch the hat to the head.

Lace shawl

A beautiful look to create using this easy-to-follow pattern, this lace shawl could make for the perfect personal present

Difficulty ★★☆☆☆

Skills needed
Increasing
Decreasing
Lace stitches
Knitting in rows
Working from a chart
Short rows

Finished measurements
Width: 183cm (72in) after blocking
Depth: 33cm (13in) after blocking

Yarn
For this pattern you will need a 3- or 4-ply yarn. In this example Claudia's Hand Painted Yarn was used in Mudslide. You will need approximately 365m (400yd).

Tension (Gauge)
18sts and 28 rows = 10cm (4in) in horseshoe lace stitch using 4mm needles after blocking

Needles
4mm (US #6) 91cm/36in circular needle

Other supplies
2 stitch markers (Marker 1)
26 stitch markers in a different colour or style (Marker 2)
Tapestry needle

Pattern notes
A crescent-shaped shawl that is constructed using short rows on a garter stitch base. The beauty of these is that you do not need to wrap the stitches to avoid gaps. The shawl is finished off with a deep edging of horseshoe lace, a traditional Shetland stitch pattern.

Janine Le Cras
Janine is a lifelong knitter who learned to knit at her grandmother's knee. After a break she discovered the world of knitting on the web, which had a new and vibrant image, and was re-inspired to pick up her needles.

Lace shawl

Cast (bind) on 277 sts, placing the sts markers as follows:

Cast (bind) on 3, PM1, (cast (bind) on 10 sts, PM1) 12 times, (cast

(bind) on 10 sts, PM2) twice, (cast (bind) on 10 sts, PM1) 13 times,

cast (bind) on 4.

The first part of the shawl is worked in garter st (knit every row), but with short rows to give it a curved shape. When working short rows in garter st it is not necessary to wrap the sts to prevent holes.

The stitch markers you have added to the cast (bind) on row help you keep count when casting (binding) on, mark where you will be turning on the short rows and highlight the central 10 sts. They will also serve to mark the placing of repeats of the lace charts later on in the pattern.

Section 1

Row 1: Knit until you reach the furthest marker. With the marker still on the LH needle, turn your work around ready to knit back the other way.

Next row: As row 1.

Row 3: Knit until you reach the next marker in from the one that you previously turned at. With the marker still on the LH needle, turn.

Repeat row 3, turning one marker in from the previous one on every row until you reach the middle 20 sts of the shawl. Turn.

Lace Shawl

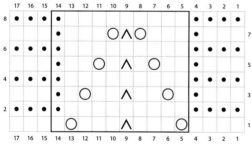

Lace border

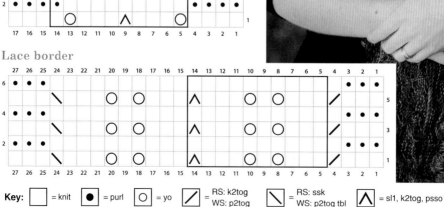

Key: □ = knit | ● = purl | ○ = yo | ╱ = RS: k2tog / WS: p2tog | ╲ = RS: ssk / WS: p2tog tbl | ⋀ = sl1, k2tog, psso | □ = name of repe

Next row: Knit to end of row, turn.
Knit back across all the sts.
This is the first set of short row shaping complete.

Section 2

Row 1: Knit across the sts until you reach the 4th marker from the end of the row. With the marker still on the LH needle, turn your work around ready to knit back the other way.

Row 2: Repeat row 1.

Row 3: Knit across the sts until you reach the next marker in from the one that you previously turned at. With the marker still on the RH needle, turn your work around ready to knit back the other way.
Continue to work in short rows, turning one marker in from the previous row until you have worked only the 10 sts between the 2 markers at the middle of the row. Turn.

Next row: Knit to end of row, turn. Knit back across all the sts. This is the second set of short row shaping completed.

Lace section

Work rows 1-8 of the Lace Pattern chart, repeating the 10 sts within the red border 27 times in all.
Rep these 8 rows a further 4 times.
Work rows 1-8, 5 times in all.
Work rows 1-6 of the Lace Border chart, repeating the 10 sts within the red border 27 times in all. Work rows 1-6 once.
Cast (bind) off all sts using a lace cast (bind) off.

Note: Using a lace cast (bind) off is best as it is stretchy and will allow you to block the shawl to open the lace up and show it off.

Lace cast (bind) off

K2 sts, slip sts back onto LH needle, *k2tog tbl, K1, sl sts back onto LH needle* rep from * to end. Cut yarn, slip end through the last st and tighten.

Making up

Soak the shawl in a wool wash and rinse. Squeeze out as much water as possible, wrap in a towel and press hard to remove

more without agitating, which can cause the yarn to felt. Pin out the damp shawl on a flat surface to the shape and dimensions given in the schematic. Pin out the points of each repeat. Leave until dry, unpin and sew in any ends.

Prefer it written?

If you find charts difficult to work with, don't despair. Many designers usually provide written versions of stitch patterns for those knitters who prefer to use them. If not it is very easy to create your own. All you need to do is to write down the sts in each row, remembering to read RS rows from right to left, and WS rows from left to right.

Lace pattern chart (written version)

Row 1 (RS): K4, *yo, K3, sl1, k2tog, psso, K3, yo, K1; rep from * to last 3 sts, K3.

Row 2 (WS): *K1, P9; rep from * to last 4 sts, K4.

Row 3 (RS): K3, P1, (K1, yo, K2, sl1, k2tog, psso, K2, yo, K1, P1) repeat 27 times in all, K3.

Row 4 (WS): As row 2.

Row 5 (RS): K3, P1, (K2, yo, K1, sl1, k2tog, psso, K1, yo, K2, P1) repeat 27 times in all, K3.

Row 6 (WS): As row 2.

Row 7 (RS): K3, P1, (K3, yo, sl1, k2tog, psso, yo, K3, P1) repeat 27 times in all, K3.

Row 8 (WS): As row 2.

Lace border chart (written version)

Row 1 (RS): K3, k2tog, *K3, yo, K1, yo, K3, sl1, k2tog, psso; rep from * to last 12 sts, K3, yo, K1, yo, K3, ssk, K3.

Row 2 (WS): K3, P to last 3 sts, K3.

Row 3 (RS): As row 1.

Row 4 (WS): As row 2.

Row 5 (RS): As row 1.

Row 6 (WS): K3, P to last 3 sts, K3.

Staggered eyelet cardigan

Use lacing techniques to create this beautiful two-tone cardigan, perfect for autumn and spring months

Difficulty ★ ★ ★ ☆ ☆

Skills needed

Increasing
Decreasing
Lace stitches (eyelets)
Pick up & knit
Knitting in rows
Seaming
Ribbing

Finished measurements

Finished bust

85	90	95	100	106	cm
33.5	35.5	37.5	39.5	41.75	in

Length

56	57	59	61	64	cm
22	22.5	23.25	24	25.25	in

Colour 1

7	7	8	8	9	Balls

Colour 2

2	3	3	4	4	Balls

Yarn

For this pattern you will require a DK yarn in two colours. In this example Debbie Bliss Rialto DK has been used in Coral and Teal. Refer to **finished measurements** for ball amounts.

Tension (Gauge)

20 stitches and 20 rows = 10cm (4in) in staggered eyelet stitch

Needles

4mm (US 6) needles

Emma Wright

Emma is a fashion hand-knit and crochet designer. She spends most days tucked away designing, knitting and drinking lots of tea. You can find her at **www.emmaknitted.co.uk**.

Other supplies

1 stitch holder

Staggered eyelet cardigan

Back

Using col 2, cast on 87 (91, 95, 103, 107) sts.Knit 4 rows
Now, work in staggered eyelet stitch as foll:

Row 1 (RS): Knit.
Row 2 (WS): Purl.
Row 3: *K2, k2tog, yo; rep from * to last 3 sts, K3.
Row 4: Purl.
Row 5: Knit.
Row 6: Purl.
Row 7:*k2tog, yo, K2; rep from * to last 3 sts, k2tog, yo, K1.
Row 8: Purl.

These 8 rows form staggered eyelet stitch. Repeat these 8 rows until work measures 34 (35, 36, 38, 40)cm/13.5 (14, 14.25, 15, 15.75)in, ending with RS facing.
    Change to col 1.
Keeping in staggered eyelet stitch, continue for a further 4cm/1.5in until work measures 38 (39, 40, 42, 44)cm/15 (15.75, 16.5, 17.25)in, ending with RS facing.

Armhole Shaping

Keeping staggered eyelet stitch correct, shape armhole as foll:
    Cast off 8 sts at beg of next 2 rows —
71 (75, 79, 87, 91) sts.
    Cast off 4 sts at beg of next 2 rows —
63 (67, 71, 79, 83) sts.
    Cast off 2 sts at beg of next 2 rows —
59 (63, 67, 75, 79) sts.
    Now, continue without shaping in

143

staggered eyelet stitch until armhole measures 18 (18, 19, 19, 20)cm/7 (7, 7.5, 7.5, 8)in from beginning of armhole shaping.

Now, work in staggered eyelet stitch as foll:'

Shoulders

Cast off 10 (12, 14, 18, 20) sts at beg of next
2 rows.

Leave remaining 39 sts on a holder for back neck.

Front
Right

Using col 2, cast on 43 (47, 51, 55, 59) sts. Knit 4 rows.
Now, work in staggered eyelet stitch as foll:
Row 1: Knit.
Row 2: Purl.
Row 3: *K2, k2tog, yo; rep from * to last 3 sts, K3.
Row 4: Purl.
Row 5: Knit.
Row 6: Purl.
Row 7: *k2tog, yo, K2; rep from * to last 3 sts, k2tog, yo, K1.
Row 8: Purl.

These 8 rows form staggered eyelet stitch. Repeat these 8 rows until work measures 34 (35, 36, 38, 40)cm/13.5 (14, 14.25, 15, 15.75)in, ending with RS facing.**
Change to col 1.
Keeping in staggered eyelet stitch, continue for a further 4cm/1.5in until work measures 38 (39, 40, 42, 44)cm/15 (15.5, 16.75, 17.25)in, ending with WS facing.
Next row (dec): Cast off 8 sts, P to end — 35 (39, 43, 47, 51) sts.

Next row: Work in patt.
Next row (dec): Cast off 4 sts, P to end — 31 (35, 39, 43, 47) sts.
Next row: Work in patt.
Next row (dec): Cast off 2 sts, P to end — 29 (33, 37, 41, 45) sts.

Now, continue without shaping in staggered eyelet stitch until armhole measures 13 (13, 14, 14, 15)cm/5 (5,

5.5, 5.5, 6)in from beginning of armhole shaping, ending with RS facing.

Shape Front Neck

Next row (dec): Cast off 10 (12, 14, 14, 16) sts, work in patt to end — 19 (21, 23, 27, 29) sts.
Next row: Work in patt.
Next row (dec): Cast off 5 sts, work in patt to end — 14 (16, 18, 22, 24) sts.
Next row: Work in patt.
Next row (dec): Cast off 3 sts, work in patt to end — 11 (13, 15, 19, 21) sts.
Next row: Work in patt.
Next row (dec): k2tog, work in patt to end — 10 (12, 14, 18, 20) sts.
Now, continue without shaping in staggered eyelet stitch until armhole measures 18 (18, 19, 19, 20)cm/7 (7, 7.5, 7.5, 8)in from beginning of armhole shaping, ending with RS facing.
Cast off remaining 10 (12, 14, 18, 20) sts.

Left

Work as for **Right Front** to **
Change to col 1.
Keeping in staggered eyelet stitch, continue for a further 4cm/1.5in until work measures 38 (39, 40, 42, 44)cm/15 (15.5, 16.75, 17.25)in, ending with RS facing.
Next row (dec): Cast off 8 sts, work in patt to end.
Next row: Work in patt.
Next row (dec): Cast off 4 sts, work in patt
to end.
Next row: Work in patt.
Next row (dec): Cast off 2 sts, work in patt
to end.
Now, continue without shaping in staggered eyelet stitch until armhole measures 13 (13, 14, 14, 15)cm/5 (5, 5.5, 5.5, 6)in from beginning of armhole shaping, ending with WS facing.

Shape Front Neck

Next row (dec): Cast off 10 (12, 14, 14, 16) sts, work in patt to end — 19 (21, 23, 27, 29) sts.
Next row: Work in patt.
Next row (dec): Cast off 5 sts, work in patt to end — 14 (16, 18, 22, 24) sts.
Next row: Work in patt.

Next row (dec): Cast off 3 sts, work in patt to end — 11 (13, 15, 19, 21) sts.

Next row: Work in patt.

Next row (dec): k2tog, work in patt to end — 10 (12, 14, 18, 20) sts.

Now, continue without shaping in staggered eyelet stitch until armhole measures 18 (18, 19, 19, 20)cm/7 (7, 7.5, 7.5, 8)in from beginning of armhole shaping, ending with RS facing.

Cast off remaining 10 (12, 14, 18, 20) sts.

Sleeves (make two)

Using col 2, cast on 36 (36, 38, 38, 40) sts.

Knit 4 rows.

Now, work in staggered eyelet stitch as foll:

Row 1 (inc): K1, m1, K to last 2 sts, m1, K1.

Row 2: Purl.

Row 3: *K2, k2tog, yo; rep from * to last 3 sts, K3.

Row 4: Purl.

Row 5: Knit.

Row 6: Purl.

Row 7: *k2tog, yo, K2; rep from * to last 3 sts, k2tog, yo, K1.

Row 8: Purl.

These 8 rows form staggered eyelet stitch with sleeve inc.

Repeat these 8 rows a further 13 (13, 14, 14, 15) times — 64 (64, 68, 68, 72) sts.

Keeping in staggered eyelet stitch, continue straight until sleeve measures 39 (39, 41, 41, 43)cm/15.5 (15.5, 16, 16, 17)in, ending with RS facing.

Change to col 1.

Keeping in staggered eyelet stitch, continue straight until sleeve measures 43 (43, 45, 45, 47)cm/17 (17, 17.75, 17.75, 18.5)in, ending with RS facing.

Keeping in staggered eyelet stitch, shape armhole and sleeve head as foll:

Cast off 8 sts at beg of next 2 rows — 48 (48, 52, 52, 56) sts.

Cast off 4 sts at beg of next 2 rows — 40 (40, 44, 44, 48) sts.

Cast off 2 sts at beg of next 2 rows — 36 (36, 40, 40, 44) sts.

Dec 1 st at each end of next row — 34 (34, 38, 38, 42) sts.

Work 3 rows, ending with RS facing.

Repeat the last 4 rows four times more — 26 (26, 30, 30, 34) sts.

Dec 1 st at each end of next row and then every alt row twice more.

Dec 1 st at each end of next 3 rows, ending with RS facing.

Cast off 3 sts at beg of next 2 rows — 8 (8, 12, 12, 16) sts.

Cast off rem 8 (8, 12, 12, 16) sts.

Making up

Neck band

Join both shoulder seams.

Using col 1, with RS facing and beg at right front neck, pick up and K 29 (31, 32, 32, 33) sts evenly to right shoulder and then rejoin yarn to 39 sts left on holder for back neck. Next, pick up and knit 29 (31, 32, 32, 33) sts evenly to left front neck — 97 (101, 103, 103, 105) sts.

Beginning on a WS row, knit 4 rows.

Cast off knit-wise on a WS row.

Button band

Using col 2, with RS facing of left front and beg at neck edge, pick up and knit 102 (104, 108, 112, 118) sts evenly to garment hem.

Beginning on a WS row, knit 4 rows.

Cast off knitwise on a WS row.

Buttonhole band

Using col 2, with RS facing of right front and beg at garment hem, pick up and knit 102 (102, 108, 114, 114) sts evenly to front neck.

Row 1 (WS): Knit.

1st, 2nd, 4th and 5th sizes only:

Row 2 (RS; eyelets): (K2, yo, k2tog, K4 [4, 5, 5]) x 12, yo, k2tog, K1, yo, k2tog, K1.

3rd size only:

Row 2 (RS; eyelets): (K2, yo, k2tog, K6) x 10, yo, k2tog, K2, yo, k2tog, K2.

All sizes:

Knit 2 more rows.

Cast off knitwise on a WS row.

Join sleeve and side seams using preferred sewing method. Join cast off of sleeve head to shoulder each and ease sleeve head into armhole neatly. Fasten off any loose ends and block/press as instructed on ball band.

Reference

All the references you need in one place

"When choosing a yarn colour for your project, you may want to think about more than just what it will look like"

Yarn labels

Everything you need to know about the yarn you're using can be found on the label, from weight and thickness to washing instructions

When you buy yarn, it will almost always come with a label around it. This label, which is sometimes also called a ball band, tells you everything you need to know about the yarn, from what size needles to use with it to washing and care instructions. If you think your project will need to use more than one ball of yarn, don't throw this label away, as it will help you ensure you get the exact matching yarn to continue working with.

Symbols

Most yarn manufacturers will use symbols to indicate the properties of yarn and give further details about it. These will often include care instructions and tension (gauge). It will also include the dye lot. When using more than one ball of yarn in the same colour in a single project, ensure that all balls of yarn have the same dye lot. This way, there will be no variation in colour when you switch yarns.

Yarn weight and thickness

Tension (gauge) over a 10cm (4in) test square

Dye lot number

Hand-wash cold

Do not dry clean

4.5mm (UK 7/US7)

Recommended needle size

Shade/colour number

Weight and length of yarn in ball

Hand-wash warm

Do not tumble dry

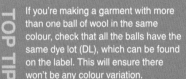

TOP TIP

If you're making a garment with more than one ball of wool in the same colour, check that all the balls have the same dye lot (DL), which can be found on the label. This will ensure there won't be any colour variation.

100% WOOL

Fibre content

Do not bleach

Do not iron

Machine-wash cold

Dry-cleanable in any solvent

Iron on a low heat

Machine-wash cold, gentle cycle

Dry-cleanable in certain solvents

Iron on a medium heat

Choosing yarn colours

You can find yarn in almost any colour you can think of, but how do you choose which one to use?

You've finally picked the garment you want to make and a pattern that you like, so the next step is choosing your yarn. Patterns will suggest yarn weight and maybe even fibre, but rarely colour. This decision is up to you. When choosing a yarn colour for your project, you may want to think about more than just what it will look like. For example, as a knitting beginner, you may find black and other darker colours difficult to work with as you won't be able to spot mistakes as easily or see what stitch you just worked. When you're using more than one colour to create a pattern, it is also important to choose colours that complement each other as well as stand out to make the pattern distinctive. A good place to start for choosing colours is to look at a colour wheel.

Using a colour wheel

This is used to see how colours work together. Each segment shows the hue (the pure, bright colour), shade (the colour mixed with black), tone (the colour mixed with grey) and tint (the colour mixed with white) of a colour. Blue, red and yellow are primary colours; green, orange and purple are secondary colours; and all the others are tertiary colours. Colours that are side-by-side harmonise with each other and those that are opposite on the wheel complement each other, and provide bold contrast.

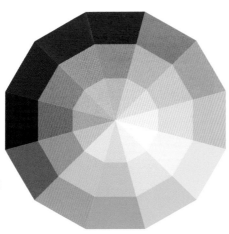

Black and white

These are not included on the colour wheel as they are not classified as colours (black being an absence of all colour and white a combination of all the colours in the spectrum). When using black yarn to knit with, remember that your work will be more difficult to see and any complex details like cabling will not show up as well in the finished piece. When using white yarn, although every stitch will be clear to see, remember that this is not the most practical colour for wearable garments as any stains or dirt will easily show up.

Warm shades

Consisting of mainly red and yellow tones, the colours at the warm end of the colour spectrum can be used to bring richness and depth to a garment. Browns, oranges and purple are also a part of this group. A blend of warm shades can create a flattering garment.

Cool shades

At the cool end of the spectrum are blue, green and violet. Generally darker in tone than warm colours, their impact is lessened when mixed with these. If you need to balance a warm mixture in a project, you will need more cool colours than warm ones to do so.

Pastels

These very pale colours are extremely popular for babies' and small children's garments, and as such you will find a high proportion of soft yarns for babies are available in these colours. Pastels also feature strongly in spring/summer knitting patterns for adults.

Brights

Vivid and fluorescent shades can really liven up a piece, especially one that so far consists of muted shades. These colours make eye-catching accessories and intarsia motifs, and also look great when used to add a bright edging or set of buttons.

Knitting abbreviations

Here is a list of the most frequently used knitting abbreviations. Any special abbreviation will be explained within a pattern

alt
Alternate

beg
Begin(ning)

cm
Centimetre(s)

cont
Continu(e)(ing)

dec
Decreas(e)(ing)

foll
Follow(s)(ing)

g
Gram(s)

g st
Garter stitch

in
Inch(es)

inc
Increase(e)(ing)

K
Knit

K1 tbl
Knit 1 stitch through the back of the loop

k2tog (or dec 1)
Knit next 2 stitches together (see page 40)

kfb (o inc 1)
Knit into front and back of next stitch
(see page 36)

LH
Left hand

M1 (or M1k)
Make one stitch
(see page 37)

mm
Millimetre(s)

oz
Ounce(s)

p
Purl

p2tog (or dec 1)
Purl next two stitches together (see page 40)

patt
Pattern, or work in pattern

pfb (or inc 1)
Purl into front and back of next stitch

psso
Pass slipped stitch over

rem
Remain(s)(ing)

rep
Repeat(ing)

rev st st
Reverse stocking stitch

RH
Right hand

RS
Right side (of work)

Sk k1 psso (skp)
Slip 1, knit 1, pass slipped stitch over (see page 48)

s1 k2tog psso (sk2p)
Slip 1, knit 2 stitches together, pass slipped stitch over

ssk
Slip slip knit (see page 49)

S
Slip stitch

s2 K1 p2sso
Slip 2, knit 1, pass slipped stitches over

st(s)
Stitch(es)

st st
Stocking stitch

tbl
Through back of loop(s)

tog
Together

WS
Wrong side (of work)

yd
Yard(s)

yo (yfwd)
Yarn over

wyib
With yarn in back

wyif
With yarn in front

[ ] *
Repeat instructions between brackets, or after or between asterisks, as many times as instructed

Understanding stitch symbol charts

Sometimes knitting patterns are given as a stitch symbol chart instead of a written pattern. Don't panic. These are easy to follow if you know what you're looking at

S titch symbol charts provide a knitting pattern in much the same way as a written pattern — each symbol represents a stitch, and you follow it to make the pattern. Some knitters prefer them to written patterns, as they offer a visual representation of what a pattern should look like when it's knitted up and can be easier to memorise. When you come across a charted pattern, the amount of stitches to cast (bind) on will normally be provided, however, if it is not, you can easily work it out from the number of stitches in the pattern 'repeat'. Cast (bind) on a multiple of this number and any extras for edge stitches outside the repeat and you're ready to go.

In a stitch symbol chart, each square represents a stitch and each horizontal line of squares represents a row. After casting (binding) on, work from the bottom of the chart upwards, reading odd-numbered rows, which are usually RS rows, from right to left and even-numbered rows from left to right. After knitting any edge stitches, work the stitches inside the repeat as many times as required. When you have worked all the rows on the chart, start again at the bottom of the chart.

Stitch symbols

These are some of the most commonly used stitch symbols. However, different pattern providers may use different symbols, so always follow the explanations given in a pattern.

☐ = k on RS rows, p on WS rows

● = p on RS rows, k on WS rows

○ = yo

╱ = k2tog

╲ = ssk

∧ = sk2p

⋀ = s2k k1 p2sso

> **TOP TIP**
> Some symbols mean one thing on an RS row and another on a WS row. For example, a blank square often means knit on an RS row and purl on a WS row.

01 Cast (bind) on
The number of stitches you cast on must be a multiple of this repeat plus any edge stitches.

02 Right to left
Read row 1 and all other odd-numbered rows from right to left.

03 Left to right
Read row 2 and all other even-numbered rows from left to right.

04 Repeat
When you have finished the last row of the stitch symbol chart, begin again at row 1. Repeat the pattern until you reach the desired length.

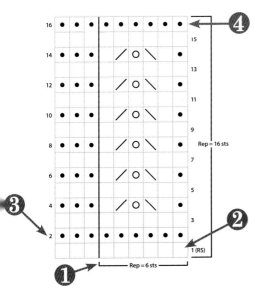

Stitch patterns

Follow this fantastic guide to the different stitches that are available to you, and use them in your amazing creations

After learning the basic techniques of knitting, you now have the ability to create a large variety of stitches. These can be used to start making your own original designs and adapting other patterns to suit your tastes. You may recognise some of the more common stitches, such as moss (seed) and single rib, but there are a wide variety that will enable you to create any number of attractive items. There are just a few examples showcased in this chapter, so take a look through to see which appeal to you most.

TOP TIP

If you lose your place while following a stitch pattern, start by looking at the tail of your work. If it is towards the bottom of your needle, you are about to knit an odd row (3, 5, 7 etc); if it is towards the top, you are about to knit an even row (4, 6, 8 etc).

"Start making your own designs and adapting patterns to suit your tastes"

Knit and purl stitch patterns

There are many stitches that you can create using just these two techniques, and most are simple to work and easy to remember. Although the majority of these will create a pattern that looks the same on both sides, those with a right side (RS) will have the pictured stitch on the front and a different texture on the back. These simple stitches are ideal for making scarves and blankets.

Moss (seed) stitch

For an even number of sts:
Row 1: *K1, P1, rep from *
Row 2: *P1, K1, rep from *
Rep rows 1-2 to form pattern

For an odd number of sts:
Row 1: *K1, P1, rep from *
to last st, K1
Rep row 1 to form pattern

Half moss (seed) stitch

Cast (bind) on an odd number of sts
Row 1 (RS): *P1, K1, rep from * to last st, K1
Row 2: K
Rep rows 1-2 to form pattern

Double moss (seed) stitch

Cast (bind) on an odd number of sts
Row 1 (RS): *K1, P1, rep from *to last st, K1
Row 2: *P1, K1, rep from * to last st, K1
Row 3: As row 2
Row 4: As row 1
Rep rows 1-4 to form pattern

Broken moss (seed) stitch

Cast (bind) on an odd number of sts
Row 1 (RS): K
Row 2: *P1, K1, rep from * to last st, K1
Rep rows 1-2 to form pattern

Single rib

For an even number of sts:
Row 1: *K1, P1, rep from *
Rep row 1 to form pattern

For an odd number of sts:
Row 1: *K1, P1, rep from * to last st, K1
Row 2: *P1, K1, rep from * to last st, P1
Rep rows 1-2 to form pattern

Double rib

Cast (bind) on a multiple of 4 sts
Row 1: *K2, P2, rep from *
Rep row 1 to form pattern

English rib

Cast (bind) on an odd number of sts
Row 1: s1, *P1, K1, rep from *
Row 2: s1 *K1b, P1, rep from *
Rep rows 1-2 to form pattern

Fisherman's rib

Cast (bind) on an odd number of sts and knit 1 row
Row 1 (RS): s1, *K1b, P1, rep from *
Row 2: s1, *P1, K1b, rep from * to last 2 sts, P1, K1
Rep rows 1-2 to form pattern

Garter rib
Cast (bind) on a multiple of 8 sts + 4
Row 1 (RS): K4, *P4, K4, rep from *
Row 2: Purl.
Rep rows 1-2 to form pattern

Basketweave stitch
Cast (bind) on a multiple of 8 sts
Rows 1-5: *K4, P4, rep from *
Rows 6-10: *P4, K4, rep from *
Rep rows 1-10 to form pattern

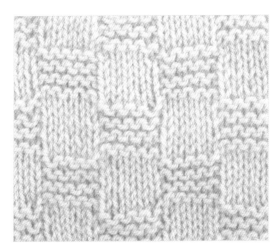

Little check stitch
Cast (bind) on a multiple of 10 sts + 5
Row 1: K5, *P5, K5, rep from *
Row 2: Purl.
Rep 1-2 twice more, then row 1 again
Row 8: K5, *P5, K5, rep from *
Row 9: Knit.
Rep rows 8-9 twice more, then row 8 again
Rep rows 1-14 to form pattern

Little ladder stitch
Cast (bind) on a multiple of 6 sts + 2
Row 1 (RS): K
Row 2: K2, *P4, K2, rep from *
Row 3: Knit.
Row 4: P3, *K2, P4, rep from * to last 3 sts, P3
Rep rows 1-4 to form pattern

Increasing and decreasing

Using slightly more advanced techniques such as yarn over (yo) and knit/purl two together (k2tog/p2tog), you can create stitches with even greater detail and texture. These form more intricate designs that look great on their own or when combined with other stitches in larger pieces.

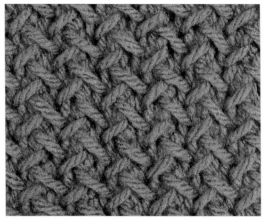

Basic chevron

Cast (bind) on a multiple of 12 sts
Row 1 (RS): *k2tog, K3, [inc in next st] twice, K3, s1 K1 psso, rep from *
Row 2: Purl.
Rep rows 1-2 to form pattern

Herringbone stitch

Cast (bind) on a multiple of 3 sts + 1
Row 1 (RS): K1, *yo, s1wyib K2 psso 2 sts, rep from *
Row 2: P1, *yo, s1wyif P2 psso 2 sts, rep from *
Rep rows 1-2 to form pattern

Diagonal rib

Cast (bind) on a multiple of 2 sts
Row 1: *K1, P1, rep from *
Row 2: s1 P1 psso, *K1, P1, rep from *
Row 3: *P1, K1, rep from * to last 2 sts, P2
Row 4: s1 K1 psso, *P1, K1 rep from * to last 2 sts, P1, [K1 P1] into next stitch
Rep rows 1-4 to form pattern

Blackberry stitch

Cast (bind) on a multiple of 4 sts + 2
Row 1 (RS): Purl.
Row 2: K1, *[K1 P1 K1] into next st, p3tog, rep from * to last st, K1
Row 3: Purl.
Row 4: K1, *p3tog, [K1 P1 K1] into next st, rep from * to last st, K1
Rep rows 1-4 to form pattern

Glossary

All of the key terminology you need to learn to follow patterns and get to grips with the skills and techniques you need for knitting

As established, as set
An instruction in knitting patterns that means to continue working as previously established after an interruption in the texture or shaping. For example, an established pattern might be interrupted to work a buttonhole and then continue 'as set'

Bar increase
See knit front and back (kfb)

Blanket stitch
A decorative sewing technique worked along the edge of fabric

Block
A finishing technique in which the knitted piece is set with steam or water. Blocking smooths stitches and straightens edges

Blocking wire
A long, straight wire used for anchoring the edge of knitting during blocking, most often for lace

Cable
A texture in knitting that resembles knitted rope, made by crossing stitches

Cable cast (bind) on
A firm cast (bind)-on edge made by putting the tip of the needle between the first two stitches on the left needle, working a stitch and placing it on the left needle. Although called cable, it is not related to making cables

Cable needle (cn)
A short knitting needle with a point at each end used to temporarily hold a small number of stitches while you make cables. Cable needles are often curved or bent to prevent stitches from sliding off

Cast (bind) on (CO)
To put the first row of stitches on the needles. This row is simply called the cast (bind)-on edge

Cast (bind) off (BO)
Secure the final row of stitches and remove them from your knitting needles

Circular knitting
When you knit fabric in a tube by working the stitches in a spiral. Unlike flat knitting, which is worked back and forth

Circular needle
A needle with a point at each end and a flexible cable in between. Circulars can be used in circular or flat knitting

Decrease
To decrease the number of stitches in a row

Dropped stitch
A stitch that has fallen off the needle and is not secured. A column of dropped stitches is called a ladder

Double-pointed needles (DPNs)
A knitting needle with a point at each end, usually used in a set of four or five to work in the round

Duplicate stitch
Made by running a strand of yarn along the same path as existing knitted stitches. Duplicate stitch can be used on the wrong side to conceal yarn ends or on the right side as a decorative element

Ease
The difference between the garment's measurements and wearer's measurements. A garment with larger measurements has positive ease and one with smaller measurements has negative ease

Eyelet
A single hole in knitted fabric, usually made with a yarn over increase

Fair Isle
Refers to both the motifs and the technique derived from the colour knitting from the Shetland Islands and Fair Isle, north of Scotland. Generally, in Fair Isle knitting, two colours are used in each row, with the colour not being used carried along the wrong side of the work. Sometimes it can be used to refer to stranded colourwork in general

Felt
Made from finished knitting by agitating animal fibre to lock the strands together

Finishing
At the end of a knitted project, when final details are added, such as weaving in ends, sewing pieces together and adding buttons. Can also include blocking

Flat knitting
When you knit fabric as a flat piece by working the stitches back and forth (unlike circular knitting, which is worked in a spiral)

Garter stitch
A reversible, ridged pattern made of alternating knit and purl rows. In flat knitting, garter stitch is made by knitting every row; in circular knitting, it is made by alternating knit and purl rounds

"Duplicate stitch can be used on the wrong side to conceal yarn ends or on the right side as a decorative element"

Gauge (tension)
The size of a stitch, so how many stitches and rows fit in to make a certain size of knitting, usually ten centimetres

Half-hitch cast (bind) on
A simple single-strand cast (bind) on. Stitches are made by twisting the yarn into a loop and placing them on a needle

I-cord
Short for idiot cord, an i-cord is a narrow tube made by knitting every row on a double-pointed needle (DPN) without turning the work

Increase (inc)
To increase the number of stitches in a row

Intarsia
A technique used for working blocks of colour. The yarn is not carried across the back as in stranded colourwork

Join
Either adding a new ball of yarn, turning a flat row into a tubular round or sewing pieces of knitting together

Knit (k, K)
Specifically, to make a new stitch by working with the yarn at the back and inserting the right needle from left to right under the front loop and through the centre of the next stitch of the left needle

Knit two stitches together (k2tog)
Putting the needle through two stitches and knitting together to decrease by one stitch

Knit three stitches together (k3tog)
Putting the needle through three stitches and knitting them together to decrease by two stitches

Knit front and back (kfb)
Knit first into the front and then into the back of one stitch to increase by one stitch. Also called a bar increase

Knitted cast (bind) on
A cast (bind)-on edge made by working a stitch into the first stitch on the left-hand needle and placing it back on the left needle

Knitwise (kwise)
As if to knit — with the yarn in the back and the right needle going into the front of the stitch

Lace
Knitted fabric with an arrangement of holes

Long tail cast (bind) on
A strong cast (bind) on made by using two strands of yarn: the working yarn and the tail

Marker, stitch marker
A small ring or other tool placed on the needle to mark a location or stitch.

Mattress stitch
A method of sewing knitting together that creates a barely visible seam

Multiple (mult)
The number of stitches or rows that are repeated in a stitch pattern

Needle gauge
A tool used to determine the size of unmarked needles.

Pick up and knit
Draw loops through the edge of the knitting and place them on a needle

Place marker (pm)
An instruction to place a stitch marker on your needle

Plain knitting
Knitting without adding texture or colour, often in garter or stocking (stockinette) stitch

Purl (p, P)
To make a new stitch by working with the yarn at the front and inserting the right needle from right to left through the centre of the next stitch of the left needle

Purlwise (pwise)
As if to purl — with the yarn in the front and the right needle going through the centre of the stitch from left to right

Raglan
A style of sleeve where the upper arm and shoulder are diagonally shaped from the underarm to neck

Repeat (rep)
Repeat all steps between indicated points, usually marked by "rep from * to end")

Reverse stocking (stockinette) stitch (rev st st)
Stocking (stockinette) stitch fabric with the purl side used as the right side

Reversible
A fabric with no right side

Right side (RS)
The side of the work that will be displayed when finished

Round (rnd)
In circular knitting, one horizontal line of stitches

Row
In flat knitting, one horizontal line of stitches

Selvedge, selvage
A decorative or functional edge. For example, a selvedge can be made by knitting the first and last stitch of every row, making them neater and more visible

Set-in sleeve
A style of sleeve where the upper arm and shoulder are curved to fit around the shoulder and sewn into the armhole

Slip slip knit together (ssk)
The mirror of k2tog: slip two stitches, one at a time, knitwise, and knit them together to decrease by one stitch

Slip (sl)
Transfer the next stitch to be worked on the left-hand needle to the right-hand needle. Always done purlwise unless stated

Stitch
A loop, either on a needle or in the fabric — the basic unit of knitting

Stitch holder
A tool used to hold stitches that will be worked at a later date. Often shaped like a large safety pin

Stocking (stockinette) stitch (st st)
A smooth pattern made of knit stitches. In flat knitting, stocking (stockinette) stitch is made by alternating knit and purl rows; in circular knitting, it is made by knitting every round

Straight needle
A knitting needle with a point at one end and a stopper at the other

Stranded
A type of colourwork where all the strands are carried on the wrong side of the work

Swatch
A square or rectangle of knitting used to measure tension (gauge) or test stitch patterns

Tail
The short end of yarn that's not being used

Tapestry needle
See yarn needle

Through back loop (tbl)
When making a stitch, put the needle through the back of the loop instead

Twisted stitch
A type of stitch that's worked through the back loop

Weave in
To hide and secure loose ends and the tail on the finished product

Weight
When referring to yarn, weight is the thickness of the yarn rather than the weight of the ball

Working yarn
The yarn that's coming from the ball of yarn and being used to make new stitches

Wrong side (WS)
The side of the work that will be hidden when finished

Yarn needle
A thick, blunt needle with a large eye that's used for darning yarn. It's also called a tapestry needle

Yarn over (yo)
A strand of yarn placed over the left-hand needle to create a new stitch